# COVER PHOTOGRAPH

It was this photograph—or rather the moment it was taken—that started me on the long journey toward this book. It was August 5, 2015, at a Sea of Blue memorial for a fallen officer.

Memphis Police Officer Sean Bolton had been gunned down four days earlier while simply doing his job—checking on a parked car along a residential street in South Memphis. He did not realize until too late that he was interrupting a drug deal.

This night, I and thousands of friends, family, community members, and law enforcement officers had just left the church where the family visitation was held. My son had been a police officer for over six years, yet I did not know a single other police mom in our city. Still, I had to be there; I was compelled to be there, though I stood alone.

I made my way to the church parking lot where hundreds of police cars from departments all across the country waited for the signal to pull out, lights flashing, in their memorial ride around the city to honor Officer Bolton. Somehow in the midst of all this, I found my son standing with his partner. I waited there with them, not knowing what else to do, and at the perfect moment looked up to see the evening sky awash with brilliant blues and reds as the sun slid below the horizon.

Many tears were shed that evening—tears of sadness for Officer Bolton's family and tears of pride for my son. so handsome in his dress blues, so dedicated t            ier.

There may also have been tears of fear for the next such event, or perhaps just tears brought on by the beauty surrounding me at that moment. Whatever ran through my mind that evening, by the time it ended I knew I had to find other police moms. I could no longer do this alone.

*Carol Carlson*

# Life as a
# POLICE
# MOM

# Life as a
# POLICE
# MOM

Guidance and Support for Mothers
of Police Officers from Behind the
THIN BLUE LINE

# Carol Carlson

**Life as a Police Mom**

by Carol Carlson

ISBN: 979-8-9873275-0-0 (paperback)
      979-8-9873275-1-7 (ebook)

Cover photo: Amanda Swain
Cover design: Todd Hebertson
Interior design by Booknook.biz

Printed in the United States of America

# ACKNOWLEDGMENTS

I didn't write this book alone. Yes, I put the words on paper, but I had many officers, family members, and police moms in my head telling me what to write. The list of those who inspired and guided me is long, and I cannot adequately express my gratitude to them. To those who trusted me with your stories and allowed me to share your truths, you have honored me, and although I will not print your names, please know that you are an integral part of this book.

First and foremost, I thank my son, Robert Carlson, for bringing me, once again, into a police family. He had no notion or desire to put me on this journey, yet has opened doors for me to create a life that embraces the Memphis Police Department, its officers, and their moms, as well as officers and families around the country. He allowed me behind the Thin Blue Line.

I also thank the command staff and officers of the Memphis Police Department, current and retired, who have welcomed me into their world, even when the culture said civilians were not allowed in. They trusted me with their recruits and officers to instruct and expand their visions of a police family. Special thanks to Memphis Police Director Michael Rallings (Ret.), who pushed me down this road, created opportunities, gave me direction, and trusted me with his officers.

Thank you to the members of MPD Moms who have, over

the years, strengthened me with your love, comforted me when I was shaken, and allowed me to share your journeys and experiences. And to Lori Mooring and the members of Moms of Police Officers, who taught me so much even without knowing it and gave me a soft place to fall.

To my early readers, who encouraged me, guided me, corrected my grammar, and found my mistakes, I owe you my gratitude: Holly Urbanski, Jennifer Regis, Karolee Krause, Nancy Purcell, Daphne Murray, and my amazing daughter-in-law, Theresa Carlson. Thanks also to my final editor, Elisabeth Hallett; cover designer, Todd Hebertson; and cover photographer, Amanda Swain. Most significant in making sure this book is one I can be proud of is my friend and mentor, Rick DeStefanis, an extremely talented and successful author whom I've known since I was ten years old. Without his encouragement, guidance, and merciless stewardship this, or any other book I ever write, would not exist.

# TABLE OF CONTENTS

# INTRODUCTION

This book is written specifically for police moms, although, in truth, much of it can be helpful to other family members as well. But moms have a unique role, one with concerns, feelings, and needs that have largely been overlooked in other books written for police families. There are good ones, some written by police wives and some by officers, psychologists, and other experts. I've listed a few of my favorites in Appendix C. Later in this book, I've also included short chapters specifically for police dads, police wives, and even one for officers, although I hope they will read the entire book so they too will know what you know.

A police family, like any other, needs to function as a unit, yet each member of the family has a unique role, reactions, and emotions. I hope that by including something for each family member, it will help each to understand the others and interact in a supportive way to build the strong family unit every officer deserves.

Still, this one is for you, Mom.

We need each other, you and I, and this book is my promise to you. We can do this, together. As a fellow police mom, I am with you throughout this journey. You have my support every step of the way and when it's needed, I will lend you my strength. I will celebrate the milestones, worry through the long nights, stand by your side, and wrap my arms around you through all the days ahead. That's what police moms do for one another.

It would be impossible for this book or any other to accurately describe the varying policies, procedures, and practices of every law enforcement agency in the country. The information provided here is a generalization, but most closely reflects the Memphis Police Department and other medium-to-large municipal law enforcement agencies. I encourage you to ask questions about your own officer's agency, as each is unique.

My first loyalty is to the law enforcement officers and their moms who made this book possible. For this reason, although the stories contained herein are true, the names and identifying details have been changed or omitted to protect the privacy and safety of officers and their families. In some cases, a story may be a composite of multiple experiences.

Note that throughout these pages I use pronouns somewhat randomly. "He," "she," "him," "her," "they," "them"—these all refer to your officer, regardless of gender, except in the obvious cases where one or the other (male or female) is clearly implied.

Regarding language, I also use the term "cop" a lot. Back when my dad was a cop, that was a highly offensive and derogatory reference to a police officer. But over the years, that has changed. I use the word proudly when I say, "My dad was a cop." Police officers often use the word in referring to themselves. Many consider it a term of endearment. So, if this term ruffles your feathers, please forgive me. I use it because I am proud to be a cop's kid, a cop's mom, and a cop supporter.

You will also notice throughout this text that I repeat myself. I do so because those messages are important and they bear repeating. There will be a test later.

You will notice too that in the case of those chapters written specifically for dads, wives, and officers, much of what is written there is covered earlier in one form or another—perhaps more briefly or from a different point of view. Although there is some unavoidable duplication, I've tried to tailor that information specifically to each family member. Reading those chapters may help you understand this life from another perspective.

Along with my personal observation and experiences, I have used multiple resources—books, articles, the internet, and most importantly, personal interviews to write this book. But I write not as an expert in psychology or mental health but as the mother of a police officer, sharing my experiences, insights, and understanding with you, my Blue Sister.

# CHAPTER 1

# And So It Begins

Congratulations! You've made it through the Police Academy. (Or will soon, I presume.)

No, I'm not referring to your Law Enforcement Officer; I mean *you*. You have survived the interview process, background check, psych eval, first-day jitters, long weeks of training, long nights of cramming for exams, and physical fitness testing. You have survived tear gas and tasers, stress, doubts, and exhaustion. Your officer went through all of that too, of course, but you were right there, feeling every minute of it. Few officers make it this far without the support of their families. So again, congratulations. You are the proud mom of a police officer.

Go ahead, relish the moment. Shower your brand-new law enforcement officer with pride. Celebrate! I'll wait.

It won't be long after the graduation ceremony ends and the dinner dishes are cleared before your new officer must report for duty. For most of us, that's when the excitement and joy give way to confusion, worry, and sometimes outright fear. Our children (and yes, to us they will always be our children) are cops now, and that's a whole new world we may not understand, and on occasion, won't like. This world of law enforcement will control our lives and emotions far more than we ever imagined and has the power to bring us to our knees in fear, defeat, and grief. It also has the power to make our hearts soar with pride, excitement, triumph, awe, and love.

I'm here to remind you, though, you are not alone. In fact, you will never be alone again. All those weeks during the academy, as your officer was becoming a highly trained and conditioned warrior of the streets, you and your family were being transformed as well, perhaps without your knowledge or consent, into a police family. As such, you are now part of a larger family, made up of every police family in your town, city, county, state, and jurisdiction. You are now part of the Blue Family—the Thin Blue Line—that extends across your department, your nation, and around the world. It's been compared to the world of military combat soldiers and their families at home regarding the strength and loyalty that bind them.

Learning to navigate this new world of law enforcement can be confusing and sometimes overwhelming; learning to live with the unavoidable worries may not come easily. It is my goal to help you make sense of the changes that will take place in your officer and your family, to manage the stressors, get through the hard times, support your officer, and even have some fun and enjoy your position in a police family.

## THE JOURNEY TO GET HERE

There are many routes to this life as a police mom. In some cases, we've known since our toddler first donned a plastic badge and handcuffs that we would end up here. I hear many stories from those moms about the small child who wanted to be a police officer and never wavered in his dreams. In other cases, our sons and daughters may have been influenced along the way to follow this profession. Perhaps a relative or neighbor who worked in law enforcement became a mentor, encouraging our teenager or young adult to consider this path. For others, law enforcement may have been a choice made later in life, perhaps after serving in the military or working in a completely different career. It can be that career change that often leaves a mother—or wife—reeling, not understanding how she now finds herself in this life.

A great many officers claim that law enforcement is a calling. Even they may not be able to fully explain it. Some say it was never a choice but rather a compulsion, something they had to do. Of course, others came to this job through very deliberate thought. They may have been seeking a career that would provide a decent living, stability, and an opportunity to give back to their community.

One thing I enjoy most, when I meet new police moms, is hearing their stories. How did you get here? It's nearly always an interesting tale. Regardless of how your journey began, I'm glad you're here. I'm glad your officer has chosen this life. Good officers are always in short supply, so I am thankful for each and every one of your sons and daughters. Just as your officer and mine will have one another's back, your fellow police moms are here for you. We just need to get to know one another. Let me begin by sharing my story.

## MY PATH TO POLICE MOM

I have learned that being a member of a police family is more than a role; it is an identity. It is who we become, whether we're born into it, marry into it, or give birth to it.

Me—I was born into it. My dad became a police officer for the City of Memphis, Tennessee, in 1951. I was born a year later, and my mother was taken to the hospital for my birth in a squad car because Dad was on duty at the time. It wasn't even Dad who drove her there; it was his partner, who stayed until Dad arrived. I suppose somehow that let me know from the very beginning that the job would impact everything about my life.

In 1969, I announced I wanted to become a police officer myself, to follow in Dad's footsteps. Dad informed me that females could not be police officers and that my only option was to be a meter maid. Of course, Dad failed to mention that in many other cities around the country at that time women were working as fully commissioned officers alongside their male counterparts. Was Dad aware of that? Probably. But since I didn't know, and had no interest in spending my career writing parking tickets while dressed in the tight skirts and pumps of a meter maid uniform, I let my dream go.

The "cop" gene was strong in my family, however. My little boy was not yet three when he announced he wanted to be a police officer. Dad—then recently retired—thought it was a cute idea, so for his grandson's third birthday, Dad took him to visit the local precinct where he sat in a police car and worked the lights and sirens. Dad even let his tiny grandson wear his badge for the day. That sealed the deal and, for the rest of my son's life, police work has been his calling. He began his law enforcement career in the military. As he explained, it's the only place in the country where an eighteen-year-old can be a police officer. Thirteen years later, he made the move to civilian life and the Memphis Police Department, following in his grandad's footsteps.

That makes me the sandwich generation, the filling between my two officers. It's a position I embrace. I remember as a six-year-old sitting on the curb in front of my school, watching Daddy direct traffic before rushing to my first-grade class as the last bell rang. My heart practically burst with pride, watching him in uniform doing his job of keeping people safe. I have that same feeling of pride today on those rare moments when I catch a glimpse of my son at work, teaching a class at the MPD Training Academy, working a crime scene, or standing the line with his brothers and sisters in blue during civil protests. My point is, I am and always have been part of a police family. I'm a Police Mom. It's who I am and what I do. I live with the immense pride, slight frustrations, and moments of overwhelming fear that every police mom experiences.

My hope is that my 70 years of life in a police family, with most of the past decade spent leading local and national police moms groups, can offer a little guidance for those new to this role. Always remember, we are stronger together.

# CHAPTER 2

# Learning the Job

Law enforcement has been described as a noble career. My guess is most officers would deny that and wonder what's so noble about being cursed at, spit on, or cleaning puke out of the back of a patrol car. But in reality, being a cop is not a bad gig. The pay is decent, and in some cities and agencies it's actually quite good. Job security is high. In most cases, the benefits provide health care for a family and a retirement package that one can live on.

Perhaps even more important to your officer, police work is a way to make a difference, to do something worth getting up for every day. In fact, there are hundreds of opportunities to make a difference within a law enforcement agency, from working with children to catching criminals and saving lives. This desire to serve is a driving force for many officers, but it also leads a family into a world of the unknown. There is so much to learn, it can be a bit overwhelming for family members who want to understand this world of law enforcement and what their officer has gotten into.

## Paula

*Paula had been a police mom for almost a year. Her son Jason, just twenty-two, was living his dream of being a police officer in their small town. He came home every evening and shared stories with his mom and dad about the calls he'd worked, mostly funny stories of small-town life. Still, there were those occasional stories of robberies in progress, domestic violence calls where it was impossible to know who was at fault, or bar fights that sometimes involved guys he'd known since kindergarten. Paula worried Jason might get injured while working these calls and wondered how other moms coped with the worries.*

*She joined a group on Facebook with police moms from all over the country. Paula quickly realized she had far fewer worries than many of these moms, whose sons and daughters regularly worked homicides, drug busts, and gang fights. So often, the posts talked about things she knew little about, and mostly she felt grateful she didn't understand the issues these mothers faced. They frequently used unfamiliar terms and acronyms, but she usually figured them out in short order. But one term kept popping up and for the life of her she couldn't determine what it meant. She wondered if perhaps it was a special unit or a rank that her small town department did not have. Hardly a day went by that this acronym did not appear.*

*Finally, embarrassed to show her ignorance but too curious to let it go, she wrote her own post asking, "What does LEO mean?" She quickly received several replies:*

*"It's our sons and daughters," said one.*

*"What?" Now she was more confused than ever.*

*Then the group leader responded. "LEO stands for Law Enforcement Officer. It's an all-encompassing term for deputies, sheriffs, police officers, corrections officers—all of the capacities in which our officers may serve." She apologized for not making that clear earlier, since it is often how the moms referred to all our sons and daughters.*

*Paula's embarrassment faded after several other moms in the group spoke up and admitted they had never heard the term either. They enjoyed a chuckle at having missed the obvious and their reluctance to speak up.*

I share Paula's story to point out that none of us know or understand all the titles, terms, information, or policies that come with this life as a police family. I hope you will make use of this book and the Appendices at the end to help make sense of the language and the job of a police officer. And never hesitate to ask a question of your officer or another police family member.

## THE LANGUAGE

Whatever role your daughter or son has in law enforcement, this book is written for you. Police Officer, Sheriff's Deputy, Highway

Patrolman, FBI Agent, Corrections Officer, Drug Enforcement (DEA) Officer, Homeland Security—the list is long. Each of these roles differs slightly from the next, but from a *mother's perspective*, there are far more similarities. At times I may refer to the differences in these positions, but generally, when I use terms like "officer" or "police" or "LEO," I am talking about any and all of the positions our sons and daughters may have adopted as their role in law enforcement.

## Acronyms, Ranks, and Codes

Like many industries, law enforcement has its own language. A cop's world of acronyms and radio codes can leave your head spinning—not to mention the various systems of ranking and titles. So how do you learn the correct words to use? I'm sure there are far more terms out there than I have encountered, but to help you get started on learning the language, I have included a glossary as Appendix A. Refer to it as you read the following chapters and also later when you encounter unfamiliar acronyms, ranks, slang, and codes.

Not all departments use codes in their communications, and the current trend is against doing so. The most common reason is the greater possibility for errors and miscommunication. In an adrenaline-filled situation, an officer may confuse his codes. For example, calling in a 10-32, which is "person with a gun," when in fact it could be a 10-33, "officer down." The response would be quite different for those two instances and lives could be impacted. Many departments have dropped the code-based language in favor of clear and simple speech to describe what is needed.

The advantage of using code, however, is that most *non*-law enforcement people, including the suspect, cannot understand what is being said. It may also streamline communications, which can be a big advantage for busy radio operators. Be aware, however, that not all departments use the same codes, and there can be considerable variations in the meaning of specific codes even among those who do. This can present a problem in a multi-agency response situation. The most common code is called 10-Code. A few examples of this code are given in Appendix A, but remember, these are not universal.

Your officer will likely make references to his supervisor and superiors by referring to their rank. Moms are often left confused as to what relationship that person may have with their officer. Moms with a military connection have a much easier time since the ranks among police departments generally mirror those of the military. For the uninitiated, here's a short explanation of rank. More detail can be found in Appendix B.

A man or woman in the academy holds no rank and is usually referred to as "recruit" or "trainee" rather than "officer." Following graduation, during their probation period and on-the-job training, an officer may be listed as a P2PT (Patrolman 2 on Probation and in Training) and has earned the title of officer or patrolman. Following this training period but while still on probation, the rank may be shown as simply P2P (Patrolman 2 on Probation). Once they have completed the probation period, the rank would change to P2. That rank will continue through a specified number of years before they advance to P3, unless the officer is promoted and moves on to Sergeant.

Lieutenant is then the next higher rank, followed by Major, Lieutenant Colonel, Colonel, Deputy Chief, Assistant Chief, and Chief. Individual departments may use other titles for some positions—for example, Director or Commander rather than Chief as the department's top position—or may not use all the listed ranks, but these are the most common terms. The exact duties of each rank may vary by department and may depend on the size and structure of the specific agency. A small town with a department of twenty officers will not need all the ranks and divisions of a large city department employing thousands.

Remember, Moms, it is okay to ask what these terms and ranks mean. Your officer has likely become so immersed in this law enforcement world that he may forget his family is still learning the language. If you'd rather not ask your officer, turn to his or her spouse or other police families who have been around awhile. This is one area where police mom friends can be a big help.

## THE MAKING OF AN OFFICER

The first thing to understand is that being accepted into a police academy, or even being hired by a law enforcement agency, does not make one a police officer. Earning that title is a rigorous process that, depending on the job and the agency, requires an average of eighteen months, a lot of training, and demonstrated commitment.

In most law enforcement agencies, training begins with the police academy. Exceptions may include Corrections Officers, who will attend their own—often shorter—form of training. Federal agencies, such as the FBI, provide specific training for the work they do. But regardless of what path they take, the majority of officers must first become commissioned in their state of employment and receive P.O.S.T. (Police Officer Standards & Training) certification. That usually means graduating from a state-accredited police academy.

## The Academy

Having been a cop's kid and now a cop's mom, I thought I understood how police academies operated. It was only when I encountered moms from around the country through a national police moms group that I realized how little I knew.

The academies I'm familiar with operate like those in most large cities and metropolitan areas. The department runs their own training academy, staffed by their own training officers, and they instruct recruits in the precise policies, procedures, and techniques they want their officers to use. Individuals wanting to join that particular department will apply directly and go through interviews and background checks performed by department staff. Mental and physical evaluations are normally conducted by contract providers. Successful completion of these steps results in a job offer directly from that department.

Recruits then begin the academy on the designated date, which becomes their first day on the job. They are paid throughout their training. Once training is complete, and assuming they have met all training requirements, recruits graduate and begin working as law enforcement officers, initially with a Field Training Officer as their partner. The first year on the job is a probationary period, designed to provide on-the-job training and determine if this job is a good fit for the individual and the department.

Not every department needs or can afford its own academy, however. Those departments generally contract with a larger city or regional training academy to teach a recruit class dedicated to their agency. These classes may be held on an as-needed basis or may have a set schedule with the academy. The other option for a small department is sending one or more individual officers to an academy class with recruits from multiple agencies. In either of these scenarios, the training academy will prepare the recruit to qualify for state certification and to perform the tasks required of law enforcement officers. Afterward, the recruit will undergo additional training specific to the policies and procedures of his or her department.

As with most larger agencies, a smaller department will likely have already hired new recruits and put them on payroll while sending them to the academy. Often however, because of the need to wait for an available opening at the academy, these officers may already be on the job and working as a police officer in a limited capacity prior to attending the academy.

Yeah, I know. That surprised me too!

Another surprise came when I learned that some individuals who wish to become police officers—many, in fact—enroll in an academy or school on their own. They pay tuition and often even room and board, while they earn state certification prior to securing a position with a law enforcement agency. Following graduation, they then apply to departments in the area where they want to work and begin their role as a police officer upon hiring, with only a short training period to learn their agency's policies and procedures.

Clearly, the requirements and processes for obtaining a job as a police officer or county deputy vary widely from state to state and from one agency to the next.

State Highway Patrols, as well as other state agencies, usually have their own academies. Often, depending on location, recruits must leave home and stay in a residential facility throughout their training period. They may be charged a fee to live on campus or be responsible for their own temporary housing. With most academies lasting three to six months or longer, this can create a burden, especially if the officer is married and already maintaining a home and family.

Whatever form the academy takes for your officer, it is destined to be one of the most difficult undertakings of his or her life. Even for the most dedicated and prepared, few aspects of the training academy are easy.

There are generally three parts to the training: Academic, Physical Fitness, and Firearms. There are stringent requirements in each, so anticipate that your officer will face long, torturous physical workouts, in-depth classroom lectures with homework assignments, and strict "Do it our way!" training on the shooting range. There are regular tests in all areas and only limited opportunities to repeat a test before being removed from the class. The stress on your new recruit is significant, to say the least.

Some departments offer perks to the top graduate(s) from each class, things like preference in job assignments or priority during promotions. In truth, however, all recruits who reach their goals and achieve the honor of serving their community have succeeded.

As a mom, it can be hard to watch your offspring struggle during these months of training, and though you don't want to crowd them, there are ways you can help make life easier during the academy months. (Chapter 8 provides a few specific ideas.)

But there are times when you can only stand aside. Offer help where it can be of value and leave the rest to the strong woman or man you raised. This is not a time to coddle or attempt to protect your child. It's time to recognize them as an adult. This is his or her time to show what they're made of. Let them struggle, dig deep, and prove to themselves that they can do this. And if you are so inclined, this is a good time to begin praying. In all honesty, even if you are not so inclined, given the worries you will face as a police mom, you will likely become so in the coming years. You might as well start now.

The day will come when your son or daughter reaches the end of their classroom training and graduates. Their emotions will be across the board—relief, joy, pride, trepidation—all equally intense. Your own emotions will likely mirror your officer's on every count. You've both come a long way.

## Probation

Most departments require that new officers serve a probation period of one year. This may earn them several nicknames—"Probie," "Rookie," or other less complimentary terms. One former police chief always told his new graduates, "You are now on the roster as a patrol officer, but don't get too comfortable. Your name is written in pencil for the next twelve months so it can easily be erased." Talk about pressure!

The stress of getting through the academy just became compounded tenfold for your new officer. He will be continuing his on-the-job training under a Field Training Officer (FTO), being watched, evaluated, and judged by supervisors and fellow officers. New officers are working to earn respect and trust from those they work with—to build relationships that are critical in the real world of police work. True or not, your officer may be concerned that any misstep could cost him his job. Given all that stress, you may expect to see some changes in his behavior and mood. There are both psychological and physical reasons for this, and we'll talk more about that in the next chapter.

One thing you should not have to worry about during this probation phase is hazing. This is not a college fraternity, and these men and women are not children. Hazing is wrong in any setting, under any circumstances. There may be jokes pulled on the "new guy" and laughs at his expense as he makes his share of rookie blunders, no doubt. But 99.9% of the departments across the country would not tolerate any form of deliberate humiliation or injury to an officer for whom they have just invested upwards of $100,000 to train and prepare for the job. It should not be tolerated by an officer—male or female—either. (More about the unique challenges of female officers later.)

Being low man on the totem pole for a while is different from hazing. New officers are, well, *new*, and they still have much to learn. Your officer will be expected to follow the instructions of the FTO and should expect to spend extra hours writing up reports or cleaning out the car after her DUI suspect tossed his cookies in the back seat. These are the less glamorous aspects of the job that every officer performs. These are also the tasks that can separate the officers who are called to this profession and who will do the job no matter what it involves, from those who took the job to show the world how tough they are or just to get a paycheck. This is what probation is all about.

## The FTO Phase

Initially, your new officer will most likely be assigned to a Field Training Officer or FTO for a period ranging from a few months to a year, depending on the department. There may be different titles or there may be rotations with several FTOs through several precincts or districts, but in all departments I'm aware of, an experienced officer will be assigned to help a new rookie apply what he learned in the academy to the real world. This is your officer's first and most influential partner. It is the FTO's job not only to teach but to protect your officer from what's out on the street and to protect the community from any potential errors made by a new officer. Therefore, while on a scene, what the FTO says, goes. Most, however, will encourage their rookie to ask questions and discuss a scene after a call has ended.

But let's be real. Not every FTO is equally skilled at their role. Officers may have different ways of handling a situation, all equally correct but possibly confusing to a new officer. Unless there is a gross contradiction to department policy, it is best your officer not confront his FTO or voice disagreement. That said, should there ever be an actual case of blatant misconduct or bad judgment on the part of any officer that puts a life at risk, most departments now have a policy requiring an observing officer to speak up. That is quite different than disagreeing with the FTO's method of instruction. New officers will need to take what can be learned from an FTO or other experienced officer and know that the time for independent decision making will come later. More often than not, an officer's FTO becomes a lifelong mentor and friend.

## Riding Alone

Some departments routinely have two officers per car, so a part-ner is there on every call. That is, however, increasingly rare. Police departments in every city and town across the country are shorthanded and may lack the manpower for two-man cars. Officers in those departments will begin riding alone soon after their FTO phase of training ends.

For many moms, this is the time when genuine fear grips our hearts and won't let go. Who will be there to lend assis-tance when a call escalates and your officer needs help? Who has his back? What if he gets hurt and there is no one around? The "what-ifs" can go on and on and send a mom's stress level soaring.

The thing to remember is that your officer is not alone! When a call goes out over the radio, it is most often the closest officer who will take that call and respond, but other officers in the general area may respond as well. Most large departments divide their city or jurisdiction into precincts and further divide those into smaller sections called wards. Each officer is assigned to a precinct and a ward, with multiple officers assigned to each. When a call comes within a specific ward, generally at least two officers in that ward will respond to the call. Even if your officer is first on the scene, it may be only seconds before his partner arrives. A call that involves multiple issues or suspects will have other officers sent as well, and whenever an officer is in danger, officers from throughout the area will quickly arrive.

It's important to realize that your officer may be a bit nervous about taking on the responsibility of riding alone. At the beginning of his career especially, all the possible scenarios they taught in the academy will be running through his head on every call he makes. This is a great time to remind him how proud you are of him and how much confidence you have in his ability. A worried mother who repeatedly voices her concerns can quickly become a distraction to a young officer's clear thinking when it matters most. Keep your worries to yourself. He doesn't need your doubt and fear in his head.

Eventually, the day will come when probation ends. For most, this may mark their one-year anniversary on the job. Your recruit has now become a police officer.

# CHAPTER 3

# On the Job

Once again, congratulations are in order. Your officer and you have come a long way. Yet, there is still so much to learn.

## UNAVOIDABLE TRUTHS

Police work is a hard job, not just physically, although it certainly is that, but mentally, emotionally, and psychologically as well. It takes a toll on the officer and his family. This explains all that in-depth screening the department did on his family before he was hired. It's a job that not everyone can handle. But your son or daughter has been selected, screened, tested, trained, and deemed right for the job. The department believes they are ready. Are you?

To help you get there, it is wise to recognize the reality of the job. Some things are just a given, even though they may on occasion disrupt your normal routines. One of the first things you should recognize is that there are things you can control, like your own responses and actions, and those you cannot, like most everything else. Your officer cannot dictate many aspects of his job either, so don't expect him to have much more control than you do. Accept these things and decide how you will deal with them, preferably without blaming your officer for the disruption in your life.

## A PATROLMAN'S JOB

The Patrol Officer is the mainstay of any police department. A Sheriff's department may call him Deputy and the state agency refer to him as Trooper, but the job is basically the same. These are the "cops" that we all recognize. They respond to calls for assistance from citizens. They rush to accidents and crime scenes. They go in first and assess a situation to determine what other help is needed.

A patrolman will talk possible suicide victims off a ledge, step between a battered wife and her abuser, pull a drowning child out of a pool, and walk into homes to find the dead bodies of murder-suicide victims. They rescue people from burning cars and hold a crying toddler while her sexual predator is being arrested. They perform CPR on a child who has already breathed his last, only because his inconsolable mother is watching. They deliver the news of a tragic death to a loving family. They chase suspects through alleyways and back yards, over fences and trash piles, through woods and housing projects. They confront drug dealers and murderers, kidnappers and thieves. Then they sit in their cars and write up the reports.

The next day they might visit a school and read to first graders, do a welfare check on an elderly woman, or write speeding tickets to commuters. They may stop to meet the new proprietor of the corner grocery store or help a new mother install a car seat for her baby. Then, before the shift ends, they might respond to a "Shots Fired" call and discover the dead body of a fourteen-year-old holding a gun in his hand, lying in the street. That's how quickly a good day can go bad.

Of course, many days are filled with more traffic violations, burglary reports, and welfare checks on sweet old ladies than blood and violence, but the potential is always there. Little wonder officers come home tired and stressed. Is it ever possible to get those sights and smells out of their minds? More about that later.

I have a t-shirt that reads, "Some Heroes Wear Capes – Mine Wears Kevlar." These men and women who work the streets of our cities and towns are, in my opinion, heroes just for getting up and doing the job day after day. You may even wonder why they do it. I asked an officer once, "Why?" He said, "Because yesterday a little kid walked up to me and smiled. Because a father thanked me for bringing his missing teenage daughter home. Because the man on the ledge gave me his hand instead of jumping. There are more good days than bad, and as long as that's the case, I'll keep showing up."

## Unpredictability

One of the greatest impacts on your life, and your officer's, will be the unpredictability of various aspects of the job. Certainly, his workday and the calls he will respond to are unpredictable, but so too are the hours he is required to work. Your officer may be called in early or required to work a double shift because another officer took a sick day. It may be necessary for him to respond to a crisis, even though you had plans with him that day. He may not call at the time he usually does because he's in the middle of working a case. Finding time to spend with your officer may suddenly become a challenge because he is either working or finally sleeping.

There is absolutely nothing you can do to change the unpredictable nature of his job. You can, however, choose to be supportive and helpful when the job throws you a curve ball. We'll talk more about specific ways to work around schedules and find time with your officer in a later chapter, but just know that every police family in the world understands your frustration and most have survived and flourished in this police world.

## Shifts, Rotations, and Overtime

It seems every department or agency has a different method for determining schedules and if or how they will rotate. On top of that, shifts may vary based on what unit your officer is in, as well as factors like rank and seniority. What I can tell you is that in the beginning, his or her schedule is likely to change frequently. So, be ready.

Many agencies are structured with three or four shifts to cover a twenty-four-hour day: 7:00 a.m. to 3:00 p.m., 3:00 p.m.

to 11:00 p.m., and 11:00 p.m. to 7:00 a.m. Larger metropolitan departments may alter that slightly to provide greater coverage during peak crime times. For example, when my son began on the Memphis Police Department, the first shift of the day, referred to as Alpha shift, began at 12:00 a.m. and ended at 8:00 a.m. Bravo shift came in at 7:00 a.m., allowing a slight overlap so calls could be answered during shift change, and left at 3:00 p.m. That was followed by Charlie shift, which arrived at 2:00 p.m., again allowing a slight overlap, and worked until 10:00 p.m. A fourth shift, Delta, came in at 5:00 p.m. and worked until 1:00 a.m., giving double coverage during the nighttime hours when the greatest number of incidents occur.

Recently, primarily due to the all-too-common shortage of officers, MPD moved to the more traditional three-shift schedule, thus eliminating Delta shift. Note that many departments use this same identification (Alpha, Bravo, Charlie, Delta, Echo) for their various shifts. It's the military phonetic alphabet that carried over to law enforcement. Lots of moms get the terms confused, but just remember the terms are alphabetical and tied to the chronological shift times.

Other agencies or units structure their schedules into ten- or even twelve-hour shifts. This may provide for more days off, which is certainly an advantage, but a twelve-hour shift, whether scheduled or due to overtime, makes for a long day. Still, many officers prefer it.

That brings us to the topic of overtime. Count on it. With most departments short-staffed already, some barely meeting their required complement, one officer's absence or an event requiring extra police presence will mean overtime. It is not unusual that an officer is required to work an additional shift or split shift, resulting in a twelve- or even sixteen-hour workday. This can be hard on an officer, especially if there are several of those days strung together, but it is part of the job. All a mom—or spouse—can do is ease the burdens at home and be sure your officer can get as much sleep as possible.

Some departments rotate officer shifts, and those rotations may occur quarterly, monthly, or—God forbid—weekly. The problem with frequent rotations is that it is difficult for officers to adjust to the new hours before rotating again, resulting in a lot of lost sleep. That can't be good for the officers, yet some departments believe it's the "fair" thing to do. Other departments do not have mandatory shift rotations at all, instead allowing officers to "bid" for the shift they want. This is where seniority and even class ranking come into play. Surprisingly, a lot of officers like working nights and choose the midnight or Alpha shift.

Others may choose Charlie or Delta shift because they want to stay busy and face the challenges that come with prime crime time. The shift an officer prefers might depend on their family situation. An officer who's a mom with school-age kids might want Bravo shift (7:00 a.m. to 3:00 p.m.), or a dad may request nights so he can coach his kid's Little League ball team in the afternoons. Bottom line: each department does what it does and if your officer has a choice, he should pick wisely. Bidding for a desired shift can take months or even years and the wrong shift can wreak havoc on a family.

It is important to understand that your officer will have little or no control over days off. For example, whereas Memphis gives patrol officers a fixed shift, their days off rotate every four weeks—one week the days off are Monday and Tuesday, next month they become Wednesday and Thursday, and the following month, Saturday and Sunday. It's a system that works, but it can be hard to get a day off that does not fall on this scheduled rotation. Of course, there's always vacation time to burn. (I say that facetiously because getting desired vacation days, especially for a new officer, can be difficult as well.)

Getting holidays off is a perk generally reserved for officers with a few years under their belts, and even that is not a safe assumption. In the law enforcement world, holidays can be the busiest time, requiring an "all hands on deck" scenario. You may luck out and have your officer home for his first Christmas on the job and then not see him on Christmas Day for the next six years. Many single officers volunteer to work Christmas so those with young children can be home with their families. That doesn't mean you can't celebrate the holiday with your officer; it simply means you may need to allow flexibility and creativity to rule the day. Who says Thanksgiving dinner has to be on a Thursday? Or that Christmas gifts must be opened on the morning of December 25th?

I know of one family that always woke up at 5:00 a.m. on Christmas to see what Santa brought before Daddy left for work, and another family where Santa didn't come until mid-afternoon so that Daddy could be there to participate. Just as families adjust to accommodate occasional out-of-town relatives or changes in family dynamics, you can adjust your traditions and plans to fit your officer's work schedule. If other members of the extended family are not open to change, create your own traditions that include your officer.

Your role in all this, as a mother of an officer, is to be flexible and positive. If your officer son or daughter has a family of their own, you may want to offer suggestions to help them see the possibilities but let them decide what works best. Your officer still needs to work and sleep but spending holiday time with her children is way up there in the priorities. Just because you've *always* had dinner together with aunts and uncles and twelve cousins doesn't mean it has to continue that way. And dinner doesn't have to be at your house; you could load up the turkey and take it to your officer's home when she wakes up in the afternoon. More than one police mom has taken dinner to the precinct or met her officer with a warm plate of food during a shift. Understanding and support make a wonderful holiday gift.

## Physical Demands and Minor Injuries

There was a reason for all that physical training your officer went through in the academy, and there's a reason he or she will want to maintain that required level of fitness. This is physically demanding work. From the moment your officer dons that vest and straps on a duty belt, he is carrying an extra twenty pounds for the next eight to twelve hours. A suspect runs, and your officer will take off after him. He will pull a 250-pound man from a burning car and carry him to safety. He will pursue a drug dealer through the woods, over fences, and up stairs. Through all of this activity, on-the-job injuries (OJIs) can and do occur. I'm not talking about the really bad stuff—shootings, beatings, and stabbings that can be devastating injuries. We'll cover those later. I'm talking about the pulled hamstrings, back injuries, dog bites, minor car accidents, cuts, bumps, and bruises. Even heat stroke and dehydration pose risks. Very few officers, if any, make it to retirement without several of these routine injuries.

Most moms I know have gotten that call that starts with, "I'm okay, Mom, but I'm at the hospital." Your heart stops for just a second, until you realize that as long as it is your officer's voice on the other end of that call, he really is okay. Take a deep breath, exhale slowly, measure your response, and calmly ask what he needs. You'll get the full story later.

## Promotions

It may surprise you to know that not all officers want to be promoted or wish to move up the ladder within their department. These are the officers who love the work of a patrolman and want that to be their career. These officers are worth their weight in gold. On the other hand, your officer may be one who wants to advance. She may want the opportunity to develop her leadership skills or work in a position that requires a higher rank. For example, her department may require an officer to hold the rank of Lieutenant before becoming a detective or to become a Sergeant in order to join the motorcycle unit.

Each agency will have its specific process for promotions, but the first step to Sergeant commonly requires a written exam. The same is likely true for Lieutenant. Many officers may need to take these exams more than once, not because they "failed" but because their scores were not high enough to make the cut. Especially in large departments, promotions can be highly competitive, and it can take years to reach that goal. A mom's role here is to be supportive, encouraging, and pragmatic. If there are twenty available Sergeant positions and one hundred officers testing for that rank, not everyone is going to get promoted, regardless of their test scores. It's part of the system over which we have no control. There will be a next time. Remind your officer of the things he enjoys about his current position and of the further experience he will gain before the next opportunity comes along.

## SPECIAL UNITS

Beyond the world of the patrol officer, there are dozens of other roles and specialized positions available. Most departments require a person to have been on the job for a while before moving into these specialized units, but once the required number of years has passed, your officer may discover many paths to follow in his or her career. Often, however, the competition to get into those units can be fierce. Small or mid-size departments may allow for an easier transition to one of these coveted jobs. On the other hand, smaller departments may have fewer openings in these special units.

The K-9 Unit is one of the most frequently recognized of these. Some officers spend years applying for a spot in this exciting field, where your dog becomes your partner, best friend, and family member. Another special unit that may be an option is Mounted Patrol. Not all departments have these officers on horseback, but those that do find officers lining up to get in. Other options may include Aviation, Water Patrol, Motorcycles, SWAT, Under Cover Investigations, Gang Units, Drug Enforcement, School Resource Officers, Traffic, Sex Crimes, Homicide, Information Technology, and more. Some officers become instructors or community liaisons, while still others work in public relations, administration, or recruitment.

On occasion, a chief or commander will pluck an officer out of obscurity and offer her a dream job. More often, it takes months or years of bidding for a position or trying out, testing, and trying again, but officers do move into various units every day. If your officer has her eye on a particular segment of law enforcement, encourage her to be persistent and optimistic about her chances. It may take a while, but she'll likely get there or find something she enjoys even more along the way.

# CHAPTER 4

# What Happened to the Child I Raised?

The military got hold of my son long before the police department, and therefore, it was the Department of Defense that got blamed for the seismic shift in his personality and behavior. The eighteen-year-old young man I raised and watched as he stepped onto an airplane bound for basic training in San Antonio, Texas, matured into a hardened soldier and seasoned combat instructor long before MPD ever got a shot at making him into something different. But I've listened to other police moms and seen the looks of worrisome surprise at the person their child becomes within months of pinning on a badge.

Many of these new personality traits and behaviors might be attributed to simple maturing, while others can only be a result of the job. Our children-turned-law-enforcement-officers now live in a world of harsh reality where they meet people experiencing the worst days of their lives. Under such circumstances, the sweet child you raised may become buried deep inside that law enforcement officer and could possibly be lost forever.

## CHANGES IN YOUR OFFICER

You may have heard that becoming a police officer changes a

person's personality, but you may not have given much thought to what that might actually look like. You are about to learn that life may, in fact, never be the same.

The degree to which your son or daughter is impacted by becoming a law enforcement officer will depend on several factors. Certainly, the job itself is a determining element. Is she a patrol officer in a large city far from home or is she a deputy in the county she grew up in? Does she work for a department that offers strong support and has great leadership that backs its officers? Or is she in a community where officers are villainized by citizens and city officials? Her training and feelings of competency will make a difference as well. Her personality and background will also be significant factors.

Did she serve in the military where she has already adapted to a similar structure and culture? Does she handle stress well? And does she have a strong support network of friends and family? Yes, your family plays a significant part in determining how well your officer fares and how much change is required for her to do the job well.

Some law enforcement agencies actually provide training for family members while their officers are in the academy. It may be a "Family Day" or a separate workshop just for wives, parents, and significant others. They may invite family members to visit the precinct where their officers will work, allow children to climb into a police car, and let you meet your officer's FTO and supervisor. Some even provide ongoing support through the department or an associated family support group. If this kind of family support is not available in your department, you might consider getting it started yourself. I did, and it was easier than you might imagine.

## It's a Unique Culture

Police culture is unique in many ways, and each new officer must learn and adapt to it. Over time, many officers fall into a world filled with all things law enforcement—their friends, language, activities, nearly every aspect of their lives. This may be because it is simply easier for them. But it can leave non-LEO family members feeling left out, or worse, shut out. It's not intentional and definitely not healthy for either party. That's why reading this book and others, as well as developing an understanding of the police world, will be helpful. It puts you in the conversation.

## Stress and Its Effects

In the beginning, officers are working under considerable stress, while continuing their on-the-job training with an FTO and being watched, evaluated, and judged by supervisors and fellow officers. They are striving to earn respect and trust from those they work with. They are on probation and perhaps concerned that any misstep could cost them their job. With all this stress, you should expect to see changes in their mood and behavior. And you should expect that many of these changes will become permanent. Don't worry. It's not all bad. Over time, they will develop common—and often endearing—traits that simply become a part of who they are.

## The Science Behind the Changes

Certainly, not every officer will respond to the demands of their new job in the same way, but over time certain characteristics develop in most officers. There are good reasons for those changes and Kevin M. Gilmartin, Ph.D., in his book *Emotional Survival for Law Enforcement* (2002), provides an excellent explanation. I'm paraphrasing greatly here, but Dr. Gilmartin explains that in the beginning, a new officer will have to adapt to a lifestyle where safety and survival, for himself and others, depend on his being on a high-alert, intensely aware, and often adrenaline-filled level of consciousness for long hours at a time. Living in this high-stress environment for a long period actually creates biological changes in the officer. Add to that the experiences they have, the things they see, the people and situations they deal with, and you can understand why there will be changes from the boy or girl you raised. Let's look at this phenomenon a little closer.

Your officer spends eight to twelve hours a day at this high level of alertness, ready to respond to an emergency at any moment. He must take in everything happening around him every second because that's what the job requires. It's that readiness to react quickly that keeps him safe. Then his shift ends, and he returns to the safety of home. That intense alertness is no longer needed, but it's not as simple as throwing a switch, especially for new officers. And even after years on the job, that transition can still be hard at times. Often, he will simply crash. Other times, it may be difficult to turn off the adrenaline and relax.

New officers especially will come home tired—really tired. It's the kind of tired that has less to do with physical exertion and everything to do with mental exhaustion. Their focus, which has been so broad and intense, now retreats inward. Their world closes in. Their body chemistry, which has adjusted to provide mental and physical alertness for so many hours, now needs to return to normal levels, but that takes time.

Often it is this swing between the intensity of work and the crash afterward that causes some negative behavior changes, such as a need to be alone, perhaps a quick temper or moodiness, or an inability to focus on the simpler (in your officer's mind, anyway) challenges of life. It may seem he is not listening when told the car engine light came on that day or one of the kids got in trouble at school. Perhaps, though, he just came from a case where a wife was severely beaten or from a car accident with two adolescent fatalities. He is not mentally ready to open his focus to the more normal issues of home and family. Your officer must be given time to switch gears.

## Permanent Traits

Over time, your officer's body will adjust, the changes in body chemistry will develop a smoother pattern, and you will learn what works to ease this transition. (More tips on that later.) In most cases, what you will be left with are a few quirky personality traits that are typical for most law enforcement officers. He may develop a quiet calmness, a sense of being in control or seeming aloof—traits you have not seen before. These are signs of maturity that frequently come with the job. He may seem less trusting and more suspicious of people he doesn't know well. You may notice that his sense of humor seems to have disappeared, or it's turned dark, as he jokes about things you do not perceive as funny.

Even off duty, your son or daughter will likely choose to sit facing the door in a restaurant. He will mentally "clear" any room he enters; he will know the exits, scope out the people, and develop a plan of action should an incident occur. He will likely carry a gun wherever he goes. (Yes, police officers are allowed, and in some jurisdictions even required, to do that.) And your officer may be quick, and uncannily accurate, in judging the character of anyone they meet.

In those ways and many more, your officer—and you—will be forever changed. A mother observes all these changes and wonders how it is possible for her son or daughter to change so dramatically in such a short time. Mom may miss the person he used to be. It helps to remember that these changes in behavior are necessary and were developed through rigorous training and further enhanced by a natural instinct for preservation. These changes keep your officer and those around him safe. Embrace them!

## The Paradox of Police Life

There is an unexpected dichotomy in the changes that occur in police officers. As many officers and family members have noted, it is the very characteristics that develop in your officer to keep him safe and make him good at his job, that can also make for a less than stellar husband/wife, son/daughter, dad/mother, or friend.

Think about it. On the job, an officer is required to be emotionally distant from the chaos around him, to solve problems rather than commiserate. Your officer must be vigilant and make snap decisions. They must react quickly and decisively. They approach every situation with skepticism, if not suspicion, and respond to facts rather than emotion. They are taught to maintain control of themselves and others and to never show vulnerability.

Maintaining this control may seem unnatural in the beginning, but officers soon learn to apply these behaviors in every interaction. It becomes extremely difficult and takes considerable practice to learn to turn these ingrained behaviors off just because they walk through the doors at home.

Yet, these behaviors may alienate our officer from his or her family. I know more than one police wife who has told her officer husband, "Stop talking to me like I'm a suspect and listen to my opinion." And I was the teenage cop's kid who screamed at her dad, "You can't stop me from going out with my friends just because you think the whole world is dangerous!"

Officers may in fact see danger everywhere and think they are protecting their families with this 24/7 vigilance. They may also crave the adrenaline rush of a crisis and subconsciously seek to create problems where none otherwise exist. Some may grow to believe they are superior to most other people, certainly to civilians. They believe they are capable of solving the problems of the world and feel a responsibility to do so. This hyper-vigilance can be destructive in a family environment and will, at the least, be ineffective.

It is not possible for an officer to protect his family from the world or from the stresses of his job. Many officers, especially those "old dogs," believe that by not talking about the job or the things they see and do, their family will not be worried. I try to let them know it's too late for that. The day our officers pin on the badge, we too become a part of the job, in our own way. We will seek the information we need in order to understand the job, we will worry about the officer we love, and we will fulfill our role as parent, partner, supporter, and advocate to the best of our ability.

## THE IMPACT ON THE REST OF THE FAMILY

Along with the changes in your officer come changes in the rest of the family. If your officer lives with you, it will be you who is impacted most as he or she goes through this transition and all the good and bad days ahead. However, if your officer is married and has a family, it will be they who feel the full impact of change. In Chapters 14 and 15, for police wives and officers, I have talked in more detail about the many ways an officer's family might be impacted by the job. Be sure to refer to those sections. Here, I offer a brief description of those changes and how they may relate to you.

## The Children

For most of us who are blessed with grandchildren, they are the center of our world. How they worm their way into our hearts so profoundly is a question for the ages, yet there they are. If something upsets them or causes them pain in any sense, we are on it. I once told my grandson I would slay dragons and fight armies to protect him. But when the disturbances in their lives are more esoteric, protecting our grandchildren becomes complicated. And we have to remember, these are not *our* children. We don't get to make the decisions of what is best for them. What we can do, however, is observe, comfort, and occasionally advise.

Let's begin by understanding how our officer's new job might impact those grandchildren we so adore. Starting with the little ones, it's important to realize that our grandchildren, even the babies, will notice the change when schedules and routines are altered. They will feel the impact of mood swings in their officer and pick up on any tension in the home. Babies and toddlers may become more fussy and require more attention. Grandma, you should remember these are short-term reactions to change and as the adults in their lives adjust, so too will the little ones. In the meantime, your offer to help comfort and care for them may be a welcome reprieve for busy parents. Just remember, your officer's family may prefer to ride out the transition alone. Give them time to establish new routines on their own if that is what they choose.

Older kids are going to be more aware of the dangers in a police officer's job. They may become concerned or fearful for Mom's or Dad's safety. This doesn't mean they are not proud of them, just that they are worried. What the child may need most is someone to talk with. Your grandchildren may be more willing to open up and talk to you about their worries, as they are sometimes reluctant to burden their parents with these feelings. If they come to you with questions or concerns, I suggest letting your officer or daughter/son-in-law know what's on the child's mind. The parents will want you to work with them to reassure the children.

Ask your officer and his or her spouse if they are comfortable with you talking with their children about the job of a police officer. Discuss with them how they want the child's questions to be answered. The most important message you can share with your grandchildren, should they be worried, is that their mom or dad is well trained, that they have many other officers looking out for them, and they will do everything within their power to come home safely every day.

In a culture where cops are so often vilified, it's possible that a cop's kid could be the victim of bullying or ridicule. A child, especially a teenager, may feel the need to prove they are tough and not bothered by the negative things they hear. They may shut themselves off from long-time friends, or even go to the extreme of making new friends with a less desirable crowd to prove they can fit in. (I, myself, as a teenager in the 1960s, felt a need to prove I was not the "goody-two-shoes" commonly expected of police children but could be "cool.")

If you see these behaviors, offer to talk with your grandchild or encourage your son or daughter to talk with them. As grandparents, we may not have the right to impose our opinions on how our adult children parent their children, but if your relationship allows it, speak up about what you see and hear so the child can receive the help and understanding they need.

## The Spouse

Police spouses may have difficulties with the changes in their lives when their partner becomes an LEO. They struggle to interpret and adjust to the changes in their officer, just as you do. They will make mistakes. Your officer will also make mistakes in handling the changes at home. Let them work it out. Trust that they will find their way through the tension, the fear, the schedule changes, and the missed birthdays.

Your job is to provide an empathetic ear, listening when your daughter- or son-in-law wants to talk. Be their shoulder to lean on and a calming influence when they are frustrated. Even as you too adjust to the changes in your officer, you all must learn to lean on each other and help one another adjust.

In Chapter 14, "For Police Wives," and Chapter 15, "Attention Officers," I cover more on this topic. Written directly to your officer and his or her spouse, these chapters contain suggestions that will help you all work together.

## The Parents

So often when people talk about a police family, what they are thinking about is an officer and his or her spouse and children. The ones often overlooked are the parents, but we are also part of this police family and are very much affected by our child becoming a police officer. Yes, I said "child." No matter how old, how responsible, or how tough he or she may be, that officer is and always will be a mother's child. Yes, a dad's too, but Dad may not be as likely to call him that in public.

Whether your officer is married with a family or single, parents are an important part of his or her support network. And parents, like an officer's spouse and children, are most definitely impacted by the job and everything that comes with it. As parents, we have an innate desire to protect our children, but there is little we can actually do in that respect. That inability to ensure our officer's safety can initiate conflict within a parent's mind. Failing to protect them from the evil in the world or the stress of their days feels unacceptable, yet to do so is an impossibility. We have no choice but to let go of that desire to protect them. Our officer sons and daughters have become the protectors now. They protect their community, their families, and themselves.

This brings us to something we *can* do for them from the very beginning. We can ease their burden by not needing to be protected ourselves. I have a whole chapter coming up on a mom's worries and fears and how we can deal with them without causing our officers to be concerned about us. I am not saying you shouldn't worry. You would, even if I said not to. It's in our DNA. What I am saying is don't let your worry grow to the point that it changes who you are or impacts your officer. You can do this!

# CHAPTER 5

# When Your Officer is a Minority

In law enforcement, it seems that being a minority is often as much a plus as it is a hindrance. But let's look at the numbers. Nationally, roughly 66% of police officers in the U.S. are White, 17% Hispanic or Latino, and just 13% Black. Individual communities across the country will, however, vary widely in both directions from those figures. I live in Memphis, where 64% of our population and 52% of our police officers, including our Chief (who is also a woman), are Black. Those numbers are somewhat higher when including all people of color. Looking at gender, 17% of our officers are women, which is above the national average of 13% but still well below the goal of 30% set by the department.

Most communities strive to have a police force that reflects the demographics of the population they serve. And while this is admirable, it does little to address the issues faced by individual officers when prejudices and uninformed assumptions guide the actions of citizens or fellow officers. Often an individual minority officer will face unique challenges, obstacles, and hardships. Their families too face special concerns. Even white male officers can sometimes feel the sting of discrimination. Whatever the circumstances, it can be difficult to be singled out for being different.

A minority officer's experience will be affected by several factors, not the least of which is their personal comfort in their own skin, so to speak. Gender, race, or family dynamics will not have much impact on an officer who is competent, confident, and respected for the job he does.

The culture of a department can play a significant role in the experience of an officer who is female, LGBTQ, or a person of color, as does the number of these minority officers within that department. Perhaps most impactful of all is the professionalism and attitude of the officer's immediate supervisors. Society in general, and law enforcement agencies in particular, have made great strides in embracing diversity within their ranks, but we all know there is a long road yet to travel on our journey toward equality.

## OFFICERS OF COLOR

Nationally, approximately 33% of all law enforcement officers are African American, Hispanic, Asian, Pacific Islander, Middle Eastern, or Native American. In many communities, minority officers may closely reflect their percentages in the general population, but that is not always the case. And even if that goal is reached, it does not tell the whole story. As I said, the most important factor for an officer of any race or ethnic group is likely attitude—that of the officer, as well as supervisors, department leadership, and the community. Most of these factors are clearly out of a mother's control, but they may nevertheless bring concern.

In speaking with several of our African American officers, it became apparent that Black officers and White officers may see certain societal incidents differently. It makes sense. After all, we bring our past experiences and how they have shaped our views to any new situation. But all officers, regardless of color, will admit that recent racial conflicts have made their jobs more difficult and more dangerous.

Black officers often feel torn between two worlds. Their identities are centered around family and friends they've had all their lives and they are loyal to that strong heritage. Their life experiences are those of young black men and women and are a source of pride. Yet they have developed a proud identity as police officers also and value the brotherhood they find there. They take their training, experience, and oath of service seriously and feel great loyalty to their role as peace officers. On rare occasions, factors from either aspect of their lives may clash. Which side are they on? And why are there "sides" that they must choose between when their truth is comprised of both worlds?

In some cases, officers of color may feel like they were hired for the color of their skin or ethnicity rather than their skill or knowledge, thus viewing themselves as the "token" Black or Asian. Hispanic officers may feel they were hired more for their ability to speak Spanish than their abilities as professional law enforcement officers. Even in agencies where minority officers are numerous and well accepted, they may be subjected to indirect derogatory comments when unthinking remarks or inferences are made about their race. They may hear comments such as, "It's the Blacks that cause all the trouble," or hear their own neighborhood referred to as the "ghetto."

It gets even more complicated when the black officer himself begins to see those statements as fact. And what about the young black officer who, on a drive through another jurisdiction, is stopped and pulled from his car for no reason before being discovered to be a police officer? Racial slurs, insensitive jokes, and "endearing" nicknames may add to his humiliation, suppressed anger, and job dissatisfaction.

Of course, there are many positive experiences and great relationships between officers of color and their white counterparts. A strong brotherhood and close friendships usually exists among all. And there are valuable aspects to having a diverse department. Latino, Black, Asian, Middle Eastern, and Native American officers serve as a critical bridge between law enforcement and the communities they serve. They may speak the language and know the culture better than other officers. They may be able to serve undercover in a much-needed capacity. But these roles can be a double-edged sword too and require considerable finesse on the part of the officer.

An officer of color may feel pressure to cut the ties of friendship with people he grew up with. But at the same time, it may be that very officer who most needs the time spent with his non-cop friends to keep him tied to who he truly is at heart.

These officers may find comfort in being affiliated with their specific union, professional association, social organization, or church—places where their dual loyalties are understood and accepted. (See Appendix C.)

Family members can also offer much-needed support and understanding. Recognizing the internal conflict your officer faces at home and at work, as well as understanding his or her need to move between allegiances without betraying either is important. Remind your officer of the good man or woman they are *because of*, and not *in spite of*, their heritage. Let it be known you are proud of the officer and the person they have become. And of course, be willing to listen without anger or judgment but with an open heart when he or she needs to talk.

## FEMALE OFFICERS

Those of us with daughters in law enforcement have a special set of concerns. Women in any male-dominated field face unique challenges, and those in law enforcement are no exception. In fact, in an industry where trust is everything and being shunned can cost a life, women's challenges are possibly more critical, even within that group. My personal belief is that women who enter law enforcement are quite often fortunate to have had a special kind of parent—the kind who taught her she can do and be anything she wants, even grow up to be a superhero.

My daughter-in-law has those parents. She's been on the Memphis Police Department for a number of years now, working patrol and serving in various units as her career has advanced. It is this amazing lady who first taught me about the special challenges female officers encounter, as well as the unique skills they bring and the rewards the job offers them. She has also provided me a glimpse of the concerns their mothers face. Her mother and I have found comfort and understanding among the many other moms of "girl cops" we have met through our moms group. I can't imagine being the mother of a female officer without having the support of other police moms.

It surprised me to learn that both nationally and locally, African American officers were accepted into the ranks of law enforcement long before female officers—decades before. This points out that the fight for equality and acceptance for female officers is not only more recent but perhaps even more challenging than some other civil rights issues. Women currently make up approximately 13% of LEOs nationally but only 10% of the supervisors and only 3% of the police chiefs. It appears there is still a lot of bias for our daughters to overcome.

There are the obvious challenges, of course, which are not insignificant. Most women are considerably smaller than their male counterparts, some even tiny for an adult human. One of the most challenging things about this size difference is not physical ability or strength, but the uniform.

Many female officers are forced to make do with uniforms designed and sized for men. This styling difference is no joke. It's not easy to chase a suspect while wearing pants with a crotch that falls six inches below your own. Nor is it a simple thing to fit all the necessary gear, weapons, and ammunition on a duty belt that fits a 22" waist. That loaded duty belt and Kevlar vest, by the way, can often weigh 20% of her body weight! However, female cops manage these inconveniences every day. They take in their uniforms and strap gear to their legs. And thankfully, most departments today have adopted women's clothing designs into their approved uniform options.

Some officers assume that size equates to strength and ability to perform the job, but they would be wrong. I've met many officers who wouldn't exceed 110 lbs. soaking wet who have brought down suspects easily twice their size and left them crying in the dirt without ever pulling their gun. Those same women have pulled people from burning cars and gotten in a thug's face, even from ten inches below his height. But yes, there are things female officers cannot physically do.

That does not in the least diminish their value. There are some things every officer cannot do. Show me the male officer built like a linebacker who can slip through the rails of a wrought iron fence to reach a suspect or crawl into a storm drain to rescue a child. That 110 lb. "girl cop" can. Often a department will pair a female cop with a male partner, not because she needs his help or protection but because utilizing the range of skills and attributes brought by a variety of officers is the best way to get the job done.

I've heard it said, "The only thing wrong with women in policing is men in policing," and there is a lot of evidence to back that up. I'm told by those brave women who became police officers in the '60s and '70s that things are much better now. Women are more accepted and respected, and I do not doubt that is profoundly true. Based on the stories I hear today, I cannot imagine what those early trailblazers endured. But rare is the female officer who has not faced some form of harassment in her career.

Women in law enforcement have, in some departments, been subjected to insults, lewd comments, and sexist jokes. They have been degraded, touched inappropriately, and even raped. They are lied to, lied about, and accused of immoral behavior. They have been gossiped about, accused of adultery, and propositioned. In some jurisdictions, they have been forced to share locker rooms with their male coworkers. They have been shut out of elite units like SWAT, K-9, or Motorcycles. They have been bypassed for promotions in blatant acts of discrimination. And they face retaliation and isolation if they dare complain.

But let me be clear—these acts of harassment are not the norm. Thousands of policewomen maintain very positive relationships with their male partners and coworkers and have gained the respect of fellow officers and supervisors. Their bonds of friendship and loyalty go as deep as any within the Thin Blue Line.

Women bring unique strengths and assets as police officers. In a world where roughly 90% of police work is not physical but more psychological, women may actually have an advantage. Female officers are more culturally conditioned to be good communicators, thus are often able to calmly defuse a potentially explosive situation. They may be more adept at reading nonverbal cues and responding to control the emotions and reactions of others. Women officers have been found to provide a calming effect, are much less likely to resort to use of force, and are frequently perceived as more trustworthy officers by members of their communities.

My beautiful daughter-in-law, who can easily lift 200 pounds and is described by her stepson as "totally badass," has said one of her greatest strengths is her ability to talk a person down. And let's face it, there are certain situations where a female officer's presence may be particularly valuable; in obtaining a statement from a rape victim or working with children or distraught parents, for example.

One of the biggest challenges a woman on the job faces is receiving recognition. As has been the case throughout history, a woman often feels she must work twice as hard to receive half the recognition from men who are accustomed to seeing themselves as superior. How many times have you heard of a man sleeping his way to the top? Yet a female officer who receives a promotion may be accused of just that. Or she may feel she has to give up her femininity to play tough cop in order to rise through the ranks. Either way, she feels she is losing something of herself even as she advances.

Often a female officer, especially one who is a single mom or has limited support from a spouse, will find herself challenged with childcare. There are limited options for the mom who works the midnight shift or is subject to rotating hours.

This may limit the shifts and assignments she can accept, thus limiting her opportunities for advancement.

Too often, female officers feel they sacrifice the most in their personal lives. Many men might hesitate to date or marry a woman with the physical strength or mental acuity to bring him down. It may be hard for a man to accept that the woman in his life might be tougher than himself. Some men may fail to understand the distance a female officer must go every day to make that transition between work and home, where she is required to be tough and non-emotional at work yet caring and nurturing at home.

It is reported that the divorce rate is double among female officers when compared with male officers, and it is little wonder. A female officer often doesn't get the support at home that her male counterpart receives. He likely comes home to a wife who is sympathetic to his long day and high stress—one who perhaps offers a hot meal and a back rub. The female officer, on the other hand, may more likely come home to a husband who asks how long before dinner is ready. These are, of course, stereotypical examples but they are often not far from reality. Many women cops feel they give more than they receive at home.

It is, however, not all bad news. Police work gives many women what they need from a career. Shift work may fit a schedule that allows them to be available for their children. They can earn good money and prove to themselves and their families that they are strong and capable. They serve as role models to their little girls. It is a rewarding career that allows them to make a difference.

One observation I have made regarding female officers is that they often depend more on their families, especially their mothers, for support. Your daughter likely got her strength and confidence from you. It was you who taught her to stand up for herself and persevere. Now it is you who can support her through the challenges, encourage her when she is down, and comfort her when she is hurting. A popular saying these days goes, "When life gets you down, remember whose daughter you are and straighten your crown." That is the message that only you can give your female cop.

Note: Some of the facts and statistics in this section were derived from Ivonne Roman's article "Women in Policing: The Numbers Fall Far Short of the Need," *Police Chief Online*, April 22, 2020.

## LGBTQ OFFICERS

"It's hard to be a gay cop, but it would be even harder if I were to 'come out,' so I just don't," one officer shared with me. He is not alone in his opinion. The gay, lesbian, bi-sexual, trans-gender, or queer officer may face the last sphere of discrimination to crumble, with thousands of officers across the country possibly still subjected to humiliation, ridicule, isolation, and even emotional and physical abuse. It's no wonder many in this population choose to remain hidden, carrying their secret for fear of retaliation.

A gay officer may work so hard to hide his true self that he makes up stories about dates with women and laughs at jokes unknowingly aimed at him. A lesbian officer may stay away from the department's family gatherings and activities to hide her wife from her coworkers. Imagine a work environment where trust in your partner is paramount, yet you cannot trust him to know who you really are.

The term for this is homophobia, although many straight officers and nearly all departments would deny it exists in their ranks. But for a reason unknown to me, some cops, raised in a world where police work was deemed "manly" work, are uncomfortable in the presence of a gay officer. Interestingly, lesbian officers may be viewed as more acceptable but still face their own form of harassment. Homosexuality is still not a federally protected class in the United States, and an LGBTQ officer could legally be fired for nothing more than who they love.

The decision whether to come out at work is a very personal and often difficult one, and the price one pays can be high either way. Certainly, living a secret life puts a strain on an officer both at work and at home, whereas stepping out of that closet can bring fears that his brothers in blue may fail to provide backup or render aid should he be injured. They may feel a need to prove they are tough and courageous. Often an LGBTQ officer will decide to share his truth with one trusted coworker or partner before announcing it to his entire department. Whatever his or her decision, counseling and strong support from family and friends may be critical.

Like other minorities, the LGBTQ officer brings unique skills and strengths to the department, not the least of which is the ability to build trust in that community. He or she may also serve well as a school resource officer, where they can address bullying or in other ways provide a role model for young gay and lesbian students and build understanding among all.

And as with other minority groups, there exist unions, professional associations, and peer support groups for the LGBTQ officer. Professional counseling is encouraged for any officer having difficulties coping with personal or organizational discrimination.

If you are the mother of an LGBTQ officer, you have surely faced other difficulties and hopefully have the kind of relationship with your son or daughter that provides them with feelings of support and acceptance. If you struggle with this yourself, I encourage you to seek counseling too.

## EMPLOYMENT EQUITY

Many law enforcement agencies still operate under rules of employment equity, formerly known as "affirmative action," or operate to correct perceived discriminatory practices of the past. No doubt, the white male officer who has worked hard to earn his spot in an elite unit or receive a promotion, only to find himself caught in the numbers trap of equitable hiring practices, will feel wronged. He may experience feelings of anger or frustration—all normal reactions to being judged and treated a certain way because of the color of your skin or any other trait over which you have no control.

In truth, those are the feelings people of color and other minorities have had for decades. It is hard to be forced to pay the price for past mistakes of others, and equitable hiring practices can feel as wrong as the problem they were designed to resolve. Unfortunately, there is little that can be done if that is your department's policy. Your officer can wait it out, advocate for change, or move on. A parent can help by giving the same support we always have when the world is not fair and dreams are squashed or delayed.

My advice to the mom of any minority officer is the same. Be a good listener, a confidence builder, and a problem solver. Don't let your officer wallow in the muck of what's wrong in their agency. Encourage him or her to connect with peers, mentors, and role models, and to consider joining the professional associations that serve their population. If you see a growing problem, suggest, encourage, and then insist your officer seek counseling. Don't push your officer to file a grievance or a report of harassment. To do so is a serious decision that could come with unintended consequences and should be made carefully by your officer with the counsel of their union representative or other professional.

And finally, seek out a support system of your own. You

will feel so much better with the support of other moms of officers of color, female officers, or LGBTQ officers. You and your officer can prevail over the difficulties, and you do not have to navigate this world alone.

## COP COUPLES

It seems like ancient history now, that day when my son, then six years on the job, lamented to me that he would never meet the right woman and have the chance to fall in love and marry. It was such a hard thing to hear the lack of hope in his voice.

"How am I going to meet someone I'd even want to date, much less marry, Mom? The women I meet on the job are not exactly the kind to bring home to my family." I tried to point out that his job did provide encounters with nice women—nurses, civilian employees, and of course, police officers—but he wasn't hearing it.

Six months later, I got a phone call from him asking me to meet him for dinner. "There's someone I want you to meet," he said, and I could hear the smile in his voice. "You're going to like her, Mom."

That's all he would say.

"Is she a cop?" I asked, but in my heart I knew, and I hid the righteous "I told you so" running through my mind.

Well, she was, and I did—like her, I mean.

They were married less than a year later. My wonderful daughter-in-law and her family have brought much love and joy to all our lives. She and my son have a relationship that works, and they are happy. They also have a complicated schedule and enough challenges to break couples with less commitment and creativity.

I've come to realize that my son was far from alone in his fears that love may not come for a police officer. Both male and female officers face the dilemma of meeting the right person who can embrace the stress and demands of a life in law enforcement. Not surprising is the frequency with which they find that person at work, in roll call, working a scene, at in-service training, or at an after work gathering. Cop couples are numerous, despite the unique challenges they bring.

Many moms who do double duty as both a police mom and a police mother-in-law relish this dual role. Our pride is doubled, but so too is our worry about officer safety. We find ourselves on edge through two different shifts or focusing on two jurisdictions. Our grandchildren have two parents who put their lives on the line, two parents who could one day not make it home. But then too, they have two heroes to look up to, two strong and confident role models, and two parents who care about the future and are working to make it better.

As moms, we want our children to find happiness and contentment in their relationships, and here we see the challenges their jobs bring. This two-cop family may provide an ideal opportunity for you to be more involved if you desire. They may well need your help, with childcare, household tasks, or a comforting family meal and caring ear. Offer your time and help where you can but trust them to work out the details of life. Their unique situation can be difficult at times, but it can also build a bond as strong as they are.

It's easy to assume that a cop married to a cop would provide the ideal understanding and support at home. After all, they each know what the other goes through on the job. In many respects, this may be true but not always.

Not all cop couples go through the same experiences. They may not work for the same agency, and very rarely would they work in the same unit. Even when they do work for the same department and have similar roles, difficulties in communication may be exacerbated by the fact that two people going through the same trauma and difficulties may be too close to an issue to see the other's point of view. This may make it difficult to offer the kind of support the other person needs. It would be a dangerous assumption to think your officer does not need outside support.

Officers even in different departments will speak the same language and even know the *shorthand* of information, so communication often is more expedient, though there may be differences in procedures and protocols they must allow for. Your cop couple likely even know many of the same people, so sharing a story takes on more meaning. But there is danger in assuming that one person automatically knows and understands what is being expressed by the other, and that assumption can bring disappointment.

When a cop husband believes he understands how his wife

responded emotionally to a specific scene or experience and fails to truly listen to what she is expressing, the cost can be high. When a husband does not open up because he thought his wife would automatically *know* how he felt, the same toll can be experienced. The wife who expected her cop husband to handle a situation one way can be mystified when his reaction at work is not consistent with the man she knows at home. Short cuts in communication are great, until they are misunderstood.

As a police mom and mother-in-law, I've learned that I cannot expect either of my favorite cops to speak for the other regarding their work. As a couple, they may know answers about one another, but as police officers, they are very much individuals. I know a number of cop couples personally and have heard from even more while conducting my research, and some interesting traits appear time and again in these relationships. Some fit the stereotypes, and others I found more surprising.

Cops, in general, tend to be Type A personalities. They are take-charge kind of people and accustomed to being in control. What happens when two Type A people come together as a couple? One might expect fireworks and, as research shows, one might not be wrong. Disagreements may abound, and apparent wrestling for power can be commonplace. But remember, cops are also trained to allow others to take the lead when that other officer is primary on a scene. I've seen couples arrive at a harmonious give and take, based on who was the most invested in the outcome. Of course, that ability to give up control is usually based on mutual respect.

Ah, there's the key word. Respect.

A cop couple that have great respect for one another professionally, not based on rank or position but on real life experience, will stand a good chance of weathering the small disagreements and conflicts that arise off the job. But then, isn't that true for any couple?

Competition, albeit fun and playful in most cases, is a normal aspect of life in a cop-on-cop relationship. Many LEOs live a competitive lifestyle, where athleticism and gameplay rule the day. In that household, everything becomes competitive—a race, a challenge, a contest of strength or will. Both my officers are very much into fitness and spend a significant portion of their free time working out in their home gym. That is an ideal setting for their equally competitive natures and food for the ego of whoever outperforms the other. But competition can spill into other interests as well—cooking, cleaning, family game night, you name it.

Competition, however, is only fun when both people win on occasion and when sportsmanship, laughter, and respect are a big part of the game.

Yep, there's that word again.

A cop couple may statistically be more likely to divorce and even encounter more frequent violence in the home. Struggles for power and control can become damaging. Stress in their home can upset routines, and anger may erode trust. These are all things to be aware of. Information in the following chapters about managing stress and crisis situations will guide you should such issues arise. But these are challenges that can exist in any relationship.

A cop couple, perhaps more than many others, are uniquely prepared to become true partners. They are physically, mentally, and emotionally geared to have their partner's back—to advocate for, stand by, and provide support. The couple, cops or otherwise, who become one another's greatest cheerleader and true friend will stand strong. Few individuals are better prepared to offer that kind of unity than cops.

# CHAPTER 6

# Pride and Worry

From the first moment we hold that tiny bundle in our arms, a mother's silent oath to her child is to love and protect him till the end of her days. *Till the end of her days!* Not just until he graduates from school, or moves away, or starts his own family. And surely not just until he pins on a badge. Every fiber of our being is intent on keeping our children safe and happy. It's not something we can turn off. Why can our officers and other family members not understand that?

I honestly thought my son would get it once he had a child of his own, but no, not really. I've concluded that it may be a guy thing. It seems that female officers are much more understanding of a mother's concern for their well-being. So, I suppose I will settle for my daughter-in-law understanding my need to know that she and my son are safe. I am thankful for that. Still, her occasional communication during a critical incident does not stop me from worrying. We're moms; it's what we do. It may comfort you to learn you are not alone in your worries, and there are ways to manage your fears. They do not have to control your life.

For most of us, however, there is one feeling greater than the fear and worry. It tells us that we, and our officers, are where we are meant to be. That feeling is pride.

## A MOTHER'S PRIDE

There have been many times over the years when I have felt so much pride in my son I thought my heart would explode. All the times he persevered, reached his goal, or took another step forward. But never before did I feel the tremendous pride that filled my soul the day he walked down that aisle, took the oath, and became a Memphis Police Officer. It was the fulfillment of the dream he'd carried since he was three years old and the fulfillment of my dad's dream—and mine—for him. Nothing could compare.

So, let's acknowledge, in every mother's heart there is pride that her son or daughter is a police officer. In fact, maybe pride is the only emotion that outweighs fear as our child, now grown and ready, joins the ranks of protectors of our communities. And who wouldn't be proud? We raised superheroes!

It's important to hold onto the pride—that feeling you had the day your officer graduated from the academy and you saw him in uniform for the first time. It is that feeling of pride in your officer and yourself that will carry you through the hard times in coming years. Most officers will tell you this job is a calling, something they have to do. It is who and what they were meant to be.

It dawned on me one day that this feeling of pride a police mom carries must be similar to the feelings held by the mothers of the fabled Knights of the Round Table—those specially selected warriors and defenders of all that was good and right in the legends of medieval times. Mothers haven't changed that much since those ancient days; our hearts are still the same, filled with pride and trepidation for our children—now knights of the Thin Blue Line.

> **Blessed are the peacemakers, for they shall be called the children of God.**
> — **ROMANS 12:18**

Okay, I will resist my tendency to wax eloquent about my pride in our sons and daughters and get to the practical side of the subject. The simple fact is that pride in our officers brings us and them great joy. Allow yourself to carry that feeling with you every day. Let it bring a smile to your face as it does to mine. The question then comes, is it okay to show that pride?

I have seven decals and magnets showing support for the police on the back of my car. I also have two blue-line flags of various types, a yard sign, and a blue porch light in front of my house. Half my wardrobe consists of t-shirts bearing police images. My son cringes a bit at my free exhibition of support. I get it, he's embarrassed—his mom is a police groupie. But I am determined to show him, his fellow officers, and our community that I support law enforcement officers.

I've had several LEOs of various agencies stop when they see me in the yard and thank me. It surprises them to see those signs of support when so often they get the opposite from the community. One officer who lives in my neighborhood told me he takes the route past my house every day because seeing those symbols allows him to start his shift with a smile. But I'm lucky; I live in a neighborhood where showing support for police officers is accepted. That's not always the case.

A good friend who lives just ten miles from me cannot display such signs of pride. In her neighborhood it could make her a target, so her son requested she remove the sign from her yard and the decals from her car. Showing pride is not meant to add stress to your officer or cause him worries about Mom being targeted by anti-police radicals. The last thing your sons and daughters need is to add worry about your safety to the list of things on their minds. There are other ways to show pride in your officers. If such displays worry them, tone it down.

If t-shirts are not your style, or if wearing "support the police" emblems on your clothing is not wise in your neighborhood, you can still show your pride via your wardrobe. There are many forms of jewelry to choose from—a much less obvious display of support. A simple blue line beaded bracelet or police mom pendant are subtle ways to show your pride without inviting criticism. Hundreds of items are available online with a simple search for "police jewelry."

Remember when your daughter was little and you took cupcakes to school to share with her classmates? That smile on her face was priceless. You can still do that. One universal truth about cops is that they like to eat, and not just donuts (although they do like those too). Whether you bake cookies, order pizza, or prepare a full-blown meal, delivering food to the precinct will make a lot of officers happy. Check with your officer or her lieutenant or commander before going to all this trouble, though. There are days to do this that are better than others; just ask first.

You might also want to ask about any rules that apply and how many officers you should plan for. Even my son, who shies away from my public display of pride, lights up with a genuine smile when I arrive with trays of deli sandwiches or big pans of lasagna and homemade cookies. His whole unit feels a mom's pride, and they relish it.

Of course, the most important way to show pride in our officers is to simply tell them. They might seem to shrug it off or respond with a quick, "Thanks, Mom," but I assure you, it's a message that every officer—every child, regardless of age—likes to hear. Certainly after a rough week, but even during the long days of tedious routine, simply telling your officers that you are proud of them is golden. Tell them you are proud of the work they do, the kindness they show, the compassion and assistance they offer, and the strength and bravery they bring to the job. It can make them and you feel good. Those are the moments to embrace.

## A MOM'S WORRIES AND FEARS

Several years ago, following a police-involved shooting and

widescale retaliatory killing of police officers, I was interviewed by a TV reporter about our local police family support group. The reporter asked, "As a mother, how do you feel about all the violence against police that we are seeing now?" I could feel tears pool in my eyes as I responded, "When I hear threats against the police or I hear of people calling for police officers to be shot, I hear someone threatening my child's life. I hear someone saying they think *my child* should die. How do you think I feel?"

The world needs to understand this. Our officers are human beings, with worries, dreams, and lives of their own. They are husbands and wives, brothers and sisters, moms and dads, and sons and daughters. They are loved. There is a lot of talk about humanizing the police and helping the public to realize they are not the enemy. My opinion is that law enforcement agencies need only to turn us moms loose. Give us a platform, and we can tell the world that police officers are human. We can tell them that a law enforcement officer is just one of our brave sons and daughters trying to save the world. We can tell them we want our children-turned-peacemakers to come home safe.

Of course, most of our officers would hate that. If they cringe over our public display of pride, they would be horrified by our public statement of worry for their safety. These are strong, capable, responsible warriors who don't need Mom worrying about them.

The thing is, they can't prevent it. It's a mother's job to

worry. Time and experience may ease the intensity, but there is no antidote for a mother's worry, especially when it is her son's or daughter's daily routine to strap on a Kevlar vest and badge to go out the door and face the worst society can muster.

## What's There to Worry About?

Soon after the celebration ends following graduation, your officer will report for duty. The worry begins that day and continues through the peaks and valleys of the job until that distant day when you celebrate their retirement. Some of the worries a mom carries over those years are the same ones she feels for any of her children. Will they be successful? Will they live their dream? Will they be happy? Some worries, however, are more unique to the career our officers have chosen.

Many moms struggle with their son's or daughter's decision to become a cop. Why would any sane person choose this job? Who would choose to go into a career knowing that so many people will hate them for it? Your officer may not be able to answer your questions to your satisfaction. There are, of course, as many reasons for becoming a law enforcement officer as there are officers, and none of those reasons will satisfy a mother's worried mind. But understand this, Mom—he has his reasons.

Joining a police department is not done on impulse. The application process, screening process, testing, training, and grueling requirements make that impossible. If he has stuck with it through all that time and hard work, he clearly made a conscious choice that this is the life he wants. His probation period allows him time to even second-guess that choice. Any officer who sticks it out through the first year on the job has found a compelling reason to be there. Trust your officer that this is where he is meant to be.

In the beginning, a mom may worry about seemingly everything. As our officers go through the FTO phase of training, we worry for their success. Will he prove himself? Will the FTO be fair? Will his FTO protect him? Throughout the first year, with all the changes and stress, we worry about more fundamental things: the tiredness we see in his eyes, the edge in his voice. Is he doing all right? What horrors has he seen? What things have been required of him that no person should have to do? What are these things going to do to the gentle, caring soul that was his as a child? How will this job change the person you know and love?

These are the big picture fears and concerns of a mother. We may not know enough in the beginning to even know what else to worry about. Not that these aren't legitimate concerns. They most definitely are, but they are the kinds of things for which there will rarely come an answer. Time will tell. And, over time, our worries may be focused on more specific aspects of our officer's job—some mundane, some downright frightening.

Did he get the new patch sewn on his uniform that he needed for inspection? Did he ask for vacation days for the family trip early enough for it to be approved? What was it his lieutenant wanted to meet with him about? Did he get the promotion he was competing for? Your officer may not be immediately forthcoming, but these are simple concerns you can ask about if you are worried about such things. Then there are the bigger things, those for which there are no satisfactory answers.

Above all, we worry about our officer's safety. This is indeed a dangerous job. From car accidents in high-speed chases to criminals fighting to avoid arrest, the dangers are unavoidable. Some are worse than others, like the dreaded domestic violence call where both parties turn on the officer, or the hundreds of speeding drivers who refuse to move over for an officer standing on the shoulder of the road. These are only a few of the things that can happen out there, and it's easy to live in constant fear, or at least with that concern always lurking in the back of our minds, just waiting to erupt. As moms of these officers, we carry an awareness that every call, every traffic stop, and every public encounter can go south in a split second.

The thing is, your officer knows this too, as do the people who trained him and those who back him up. This danger is exactly what our officers are trained for. That officer on the street is not the child you raised. And it's not just that he or she is now an adult, although that is certainly an important factor. Skilled training officers have, by now, made him something more. Your officer knows things and can do things that you never imagined. He is stronger, smarter, and more capable than you can possibly realize. Trust in that!

Most of us do know our sons or daughters are trained and ready professionals. We remind ourselves of that often. We act all cool about the dangers they face, even tell our officers that we have complete confidence in them, as we should. But this is just us here—moms who know and understand. Here, together, we can admit we are worried. Some of us in fact are truly frightened. But know this—those are *our* feelings. You don't get to put those feelings on your officer. He or she is not responsible for our fears. Those are *our* emotions to manage.

## MANAGING OUR FEARS

With so much that can go wrong, it's completely natural that a parent worries. That worry will stay with you as long as you have an officer on the job, but it does not have to interfere with your life. You have the power to control it. Don't let it become a burden to you, and again, especially not to your officer.

It's true, when public sentiment turns against police officers or threats are made against them, a mother or father can become filled with fear. But your officer is aware of the threat and prepared to deal with it. He doesn't need your fear in his head while working a job that requires full focus. Instead, protect your officer from the stress of your worries. This is where parents need to remind themselves to show strength, calm, and confidence, at least to their officer. It may not be how you feel at the moment, but it should be how you act. Consider it a gift to your officer.

So, how do you do that? And is it possible for that calm to become how you really feel? My mother, many years ago when faced with my occasional snarky attitude, would tell me to change my outlook by suggesting that I "fake it till you feel it." That might work here, but let's see if we can find a few ways for you to genuinely find that sense of calm and confidence that will allow you to relax a bit.

Your officer, sensing your concern, will likely assure you that he will be fine, that he can handle any situation, and his partners will respond to any call for assistance. Believe him. In all my years following critical incidents involving police officers, never once have I heard of an officer getting hurt because he didn't *know* what to do. If you think back to all those weeks of academy training, when your officer would come home exhausted and spend long hours studying, those were the days when he was learning how to handle potentially dangerous situations.

Recruits work scenarios that prepare them for the unexpected. During the FTO phase, your officer rode with a field training officer so he could observe and learn and practice in the real world. Your officer was not put on the street in a patrol car until his training officer determined he was ready. And no officer, new or twenty-year veteran, is left without planned backup. Trust your officer when he tells you he can handle the job. Remember, your officer trusts his training, his partner, and his backup. You can too.

*If they are brave enough to do this job, we have to be brave enough to let them.*

—AUTHOR UNKNOWN

## What *Can* We Do and *Not* Do?

Many parents will say, "Okay, sure, I trust her and her training and her fellow officers, but I'd feel better if I could *do* something. Isn't there something I can do to help keep her safe or at least to reduce my worries?" Sure there is, but first let's look at some things we *shouldn't* do.

There are many positive ways to manage your fears, short of driving around her jurisdiction looking for your officer's car to see if she is safe or calling fifteen times during a shift to be sure she's still alive. And yes, I know moms and dads who have done both. Just don't.

Also, don't call the chief to tell him you believe your officer is tired, stressed, or pushed too hard and needs a break. Don't file a complaint against your officer's FTO or academy instructor. Yep, I've known that mom as well. Just don't do that stuff. Don't be *that* mom. I promise you, interfering in your officer's career will alienate them and quite possibly cost him or her more than mere embarrassment. Remember, managing your worries is on *you*.

So, what are some *good* things we *can* do for our officers? Let's start with your graduation gift when your officer leaves the academy—or birthday and other special occasion gifts, if graduation is in your rearview mirror. There are several items that your officer might like to have on the job that will increase his or her safety. I've included a comprehensive list of gift ideas in Appendix D, but here are just a few suggestions. Perhaps a high quality and *approved* backup gun would be appreciated by your officer. Most departments provide a list of approved personal weapons that officers may carry. Good boots, Kevlar-lined gloves, and cold weather clothing all are important to an officer's safety as well. Sometimes moms feel better knowing they have provided their officer the best equipment available.

For the mom who can't sleep at night because her officer works late and her nights are consumed with visions of all the dangers he is facing, it might help to know when your officer is off duty and headed home. It is completely reasonable to ask for a quick text just letting you know his shift has ended. Just "I'm off now" is all that's needed.

I recall one officer who agreed to call his mother after each shift just so she could hear his voice, and it turned into something much more. What for him began as a slightly annoying quick call he had to make grew into a regular late night conversation that both enjoyed and benefitted from. Most nights they just talked about random things, family stuff, or a funny story but, on occasion, the calls allowed the officer to talk out a rough call he'd had. Even when the stories were hard to hear, this mom knew her son was safe—he was, after all, on the phone talking to her at 1:30 in the morning—and she found peace. Keep in mind, however, the point is not to have a long conversation but just to get that quick message saying his shift is over. That is all you really need to put your mind at ease.

One of the things that helped me most, and still does to this day, is knowledge. Whether my son is deployed with the military (his second job) or working a riot in downtown Memphis, I've found that the more I know, the better I can handle a situation. He doesn't understand this, of course, but usually he or his wife will tell me basic information to satisfy my need to know. I also watch the news and follow social media to stay up to date on current events. For me, the more I know and understand about my son's job and his current situation, the more relaxed I feel. What I absolutely don't do—and never recommend—is listening to a police scanner.

Our department blocks public access to radio communications, although I do know of some people who have managed to get into the system. The problem with listening to a police scanner is that it provides such a small fraction of information it can often be misinterpreted. It's like watching a circus through a single peephole. You miss most of the action and have no idea what is actually happening on a scene. It can scare a mom to her core or leave her completely in the dark.

Yes, I know parents in other cities and towns who listen to their scanners nightly, and in a small community it may be more easily followed, but I still don't recommend it. Would you want someone in your family listening in on you at work? Listening for your officer's voice over the police scanner is, in my opinion, just a small step away from that crazy mom who drives around all night watching him work. Just don't do it.

For me and many parents, learning about our officer's job and department goes a long way toward putting us at ease. Reading this book is a good start, but try to learn what you can about your local department. A lot of that knowledge will come with time, but you can be proactive too. Attend community events put on by the department. Learn about the philosophy under which they operate. Meet other officers and their commanders. Look up your department's website. Yes, they usually have one, and it's filled with helpful information about the various internal departments, special units, coverage areas, and precincts.

Having said all this about my desire for knowledge, some moms prefer just the opposite, and that's perfectly okay too. Many moms, and wives as well, simply don't want to know anything about the job or what might be going on in their city that their officer may be responding to. You need to figure out where you are in this desire for information. If you have nightmares about every burglary or shooting your son or daughter tells you about, let them know that you are not the right person to share those stories with. If the local news makes you sick to your stomach, stop watching it.

You might still want to drop by the station with goodies on occasion, but you don't have to walk past the equipment room or sit in the break room listening to war stories. You are responsible for identifying and maintaining your comfort level, and you can do so without drawing attention to your worries.

You can also pray for your officer. For many, prayer is the most calming thing you can do. As I mentioned earlier, even if you have not been so inclined in the past and regardless of your faith or beliefs, it may bring comfort now. You may even want to give your officer a St. Michael pendant to wear under his uniform. St. Michael is the patron saint of peace officers around the world. You would be surprised at the number of officers who wear this pendant and are bolstered by the message of love it brings them.

Many police moms have found they feel much more relaxed after meeting their officer's partner and fellow officers. This is one more benefit of visiting your son's or daughter's precinct to deliver treats. It's not only a great way to thank officers for the work they do, but it also provides an opportunity to see who it is that has your officer's six (see the glossary in Appendix A: Got Your Six).

I know one mom who started sending little treats and gifts with her son on a regular basis that were specifically for his partner. Even though she had never actually met her son's partner, she would put cookies, brownies, or other goodies in a bag for her son to pass along. This went on for quite some time before she finally met the man her son rode with. Upon their meeting, the officer thanked her for the gifts, and out of sincere curiosity, asked why she had been doing this for him. She explained that it was so he might think of her and feel more obligated to step in to help her son if it was ever needed. (Note, bribery is *not* necessary to know that officers will be there for one another.)

## Not Your Officer's Responsibility

Whatever way you find to put your mind at rest, that is your task. I repeat this, because it is important. It is not your officer's responsibility to prevent you from worrying. As parents, we have to realize that this is their life, their career. Our officers are highly trained professionals, and they are well prepared to do their job. Our job is to support them and let them know we believe in them. Our job is to tell them we are proud of them.

# THE EXCEPTION TO THE RULE

There is one scenario, however, when I put the responsibility on the officer to ease a mom's fears. It doesn't happen very often in most departments, but when it does, a mother has very little control over what she hears. This means her maternal instincts take over—they go into overdrive, and she has little recourse other than to turn to her officer for reassurance.

In most cities, whenever there is an "officer down" call, the media will be on top of the story in less than five minutes. Within ten minutes, television stations are breaking into regular programming to announce the incident. Wherever a police mom happens to be, she is likely to hear about it on TV, on Facebook, or from a co-worker or neighbor. Of course, that early on, the media will not have details. No names will be released. What a police mom hears is just that an officer has been critically wounded or killed. With that, it's the unknown that becomes terrifying. She needs to know it was not her child. But Mom, you cannot panic.

You need to understand that your officer is likely going to be very busy, even if not directly involved. Dozens of officers will be called to the scene right away. There's a crime scene to protect, a suspect to be caught. An investigation will begin immediately. The officer will be transported to the hospital under police motorcade and officers will stand by at the hospital in a show of support and solidarity. The family will be protected, consoled, and comforted. Officers will stand in support of one another. And during all of this, every officer's mom is anxiously awaiting news. The only thing she doesn't know is how or when that news will reach her.

In this scenario, a mom's first response is to call her officer. He likely won't answer. So she will want to call again—and again—and again. She may even want to call his precinct or the police chief. *Stop!* You cannot expect your officer or anyone in the department to take your calls. They are busy. They are doing what needs to be done in that moment. This is when you and your officer need to have a plan in place.

Talk to your officer about the possibility of such an event occurring. Tell them you have no intention of panicking should an officer within their department get injured, but they must play a role in your remaining calm. Ask your officer to contact you to let you know they are safe as soon as it's possible to do so. All you're asking is for a quick text or phone call saying, "I'm okay." The rest of the story can come later. Your officer can then get back to the task at hand. *This* is a reasonable request from a police mom.

When I do presentations for new recruits at the police academy, I always go over this with the starry-eyed soon-to-be officers before me. Then, in the new family orientations that follow graduation, I tell the parents the same thing. This is the *one* time that an officer has responsibility for protecting his mom from stark terror. This *one* time, they are told, CALL YOUR MOM!

# CHAPTER 7

# Living by the Rules

Y ou've probably realized by now that having a police officer in the family can upset routines and make life a bit more complicated. As one young teenager said, or rather yelled, to her dad during his first year on the job, "You've gone and ruined everything!" Teenagers can be a bit dramatic. But in all seriousness, police work doesn't have to ruin everything, although it can be disruptive to the status quo. And you, Mom, want to make things better for your family. How can you help make this new life work?

It's important to realize it's not entirely up to you. A police family, like any other family, needs to work as a cohesive unit. The more people in a family, the harder that may be. You can hopefully play a role by offering solutions without stepping on too many toes, but all family members will need to work together. Your officer son or daughter will have a role in making it work as well, but they will appreciate not having to solve every problem alone.

My suggestion is to start with a set of ground rules—agreements that can be put in place and never questioned or forgotten. Within this framework, each family member can be assured that they have stability and safety. Each family will determine their own ground rules, but in the following section we will look at a few that you may want to consider.

## ESTABLISHING GROUND RULES

Just as preplanning can help for crisis situations (more about that later), it can make daily life go much more smoothly as well. Setting ground rules means making a plan, or a promise, of how a family will operate. Whereas the individual needs of family members will change over time, the ground rules stay basically the same. And ground rules apply to everyone, from the youngest to the oldest. They are what everyone can count on. Your family will create your own, of course, but I'm going to lay out a few basic suggestions.

### Everyone's Needs are Heard and Considered

When I was still quite young, I adored seeing my dad in uniform. I thought he was the most handsome officer and greatest protector the world had ever known. But what comforted me most when he came home in the evening was seeing him transform back into my daddy.

My mom, sisters, and I would all greet him when he came in the door, and I would then follow him into my parents' bedroom. I watched as he removed his gun and put it on the top closet shelf. He then pulled off the handcuffs clipped to his belt, removed the badge from his shirt, and dropped his duty belt on the bed. I felt reassured, as I watched him change back into plain ol' Daddy. He was home and all was good. It was a silly thing, of course, to want to watch this transformation, but it was what this five-year-old needed at the time.

And even now, some sixty-five years later, I recall the conversations we had during those few minutes spent alone together each day. I would hold his badge in my hands as he told me about his day, and I would play with the handcuffs while telling him about school or my latest adventures. Daddy always made me laugh with silly faces and funny jokes. I eventually outgrew this need or got busy with other things. I don't remember when it ended. But for a time, I had Daddy to myself every evening as he changed persona. Yet, even in casual clothes, he was still my hero.

That's what this is about. Making room for each person in the family, each child, spouse, and parent. Making space for your officer to find love and support from his family. Making time for memories to be built that provide each family member with a feeling of belonging. These are the things that matter when one family member has a job that puts him or her in danger each day, a job that at any time could throw everyone's life into turmoil. Make a promise—or rule, if you will—that every person in the family matters and will be heard; an agreement that the needs of each family member will be considered. That's a rule that will benefit your whole family.

## Honesty

Every member of the family should give themselves a good hard look and come to know their genuine feelings and needs. They must then make a commitment to be honest about those things with the ones they love. I don't mean that a worried police mom needs to tell her grandchildren she is afraid something terrible will happen to their mommy, or even that she should tell her LEO daughter that she lies awake at night, fretting over what could happen. I refer instead to that police mom being honest with her officer if, in fact, hearing about the danger and horrific experiences that come with the job cause her unnecessary anxiety. I'm talking about an officer being truthful about needing an hour alone to decompress, or a wife speaking up if she needs more help around the house, or a child telling his parents that he is being bullied at school.

I'm not just talking about being honest about what each person needs, but also about how they feel. A child should know it's okay to be honest if they feel hurt that dad missed the school play. A wife needs to know she can tell her husband that she is lonely. A mom should be able to share her desire to spend time with her son. Whatever a person is feeling is safe to share if the ground rules say they should be honest.

A rule of honesty also relieves family members from having to guess what their loved one is thinking. In a family where time together is often cut short, no one wants to waste it playing guessing games. Just agree to be honest with what you are thinking and feeling. Agree to share your needs and desires. And agree to accept one another's truth and trust with respect.

## Respect

You're going to hear me use this word a lot throughout this book. It's kind of important. But what does it mean in a police family? It's probably not much different than in any other, I suppose, but for our purposes, it serves as the catch-all ground rule for life in a police family.

It embodies the previous sections on making sure every person in a family is heard and that they are able to be honest about feelings and needs. It is perhaps the most important ground rule any family can have. Respect within a family ensures emotional safety and, without it, there can be no trust. Even small children know when they are not respected, although they may not have a word for it yet.

I frequently hear these days that the problem with society is a lack of respect—for other people, for differing opinions, for authority, and even for oneself. While society debates how to bring back respect, why don't we just initiate it within our own families? Surely we can have respect for one another there. It means listening, accepting, and showing compassion. Young children will learn respect by seeing it modeled at home as we listen to each other's opinions, accept our differences, honor our needs, offer compassion, and literally care for one another.

Of all the ground rules and guidelines, this is by far the most important.

That's it. As far as ground rules go, that is really all that is needed. You may have others in mind that are important to your family, so feel free to build on this. Just remember that these ground rules are the permanent rules that meet the most fundamental needs of a family. Other family rules and guidelines can be created and agreed upon as needed at any point as your police family grows.

## GUIDELINES AND AGREEMENTS

Over time, many of the rules or agreements you put in place now will change. Officers will get married (or divorced), parents will get older, children will grow up , and the things that seemed important at one time will no longer matter. The ground rules, however, will remain the same. But let's talk for a bit about some of the other things that may be important to you now, things about which you might want to reach an understanding.

### Communication

I'm not telling you anything new when I say communication is critical for a healthy family environment. You may not yet realize, however, just how challenging open and honest communication is for a police family. With an officer working long hours and strange shifts, even simple face-to-face conversation can be difficult at times.

Establishing a baseline expectation for communication may help to ensure that you and your officer stay connected and that you are not left out of family news from your officer's spouse or children. This is especially valuable if your officer lives too far away for regular visits. Establish a good time for everyone, maybe Sunday evening or whenever their busy schedules allow, and make a weekly phone call. Catch up on what's happening in everyone's life. These regular phone calls can become treasured traditions and happy memories for all.

Remember too that technology provides opportunities for video calls, group chats, and other ways to communicate with those you love, whether they are across town or across the country.

## Sharing Job-Related Details

Speaking of communication and honesty, it's also important to communicate regarding your comfort level with some of the job-related details your officer may share. We have mentioned the importance of your officer's being able to talk about his job, to unload and work through the difficult things he has seen and done. But that person with whom your officer shares the painful and horrific aspects of the job does not have to be you.

It absolutely should not be you if that information is going to leave you upset and stressed. It may be helpful to come to an agreement about what you can handle and what should not be shared with you.

I know several police moms who have *wanted* to be that trusted person her officer could talk to and cry with, and several have tried hard to offer that, only to learn they are not cut out for it. It is impossible to imagine every scenario and how you might feel upon hearing these stories, but if you know—or discover along the way—that you cannot handle the details your officer may share, admit that to yourself and tell your officer. Oftentimes, a better listener can be found in Dad, a sibling, or a close friend outside the department.

All that said, there will be days when your officer will face situations that rock him to the core and a different "rule" needs to be used. It may be a time when he narrowly escapes with his life or is forced to take the life of a perpetrator. Perhaps it will be a time when he is put on administrative leave because of a traumatic scene he worked. There may be a particular call that your officer simply can't get past or an accumulation of traumatic events that leave your officer in need of help. These may be times when he truly needs to talk to Mom.

Should that time ever come, you will want your officer to talk to you about what they are facing despite whatever stress it may cause you. If you have not thought to communicate that commitment to be available for your officer on those occasions, he or she may feel a need to protect you even at a time when they need you the most.

I've gotten stories of horrendous car accidents, victims in dire trouble, emotional feel-good moments, and the infamous, "I'm okay, but..." phone call from the hospital. I've told my son I'm here to listen anytime he wants to call me. Over the years his stories, both bad and good, have dwindled to mostly amusing anecdotes about the job, but still, he knows I'm here. That's what matters most.

If your officer has a spouse or significant other, encourage that loved one to be equally honest with themselves and their officer about what they want to hear and don't. All adults in the family need to ask themselves these same questions and share their desires and comfort levels. Your officer deserves to know where they stand and to whom he or she can talk. You can encourage support for your officer through open communication among all family members.

## Guns

I grew up in a different era. Teenage boys drove pickup trucks to school with their shotguns displayed in the back windows, and kids never considered a real gun a toy because we all had cap shooters (yes, even the girls) and we knew the difference. My dad was a cop and a gunsmith. His guns were not in a safe, and the only one kept out of our reach was his service revolver. When he said, "Don't touch the guns," it never occurred to us to disobey.

This rule was so ingrained into my sisters and I that we were unwilling to break it even when *not* doing so meant getting in trouble. I recall the day when both Mom and Dad were at work and my older sister was in charge. We were roughhousing and running through the house when we accidentally banged into my parents' bedroom door. We immediately realized we'd hit the five or six rifles Dad kept stored behind the door. The entire stack of rifles crashed to the floor, one even skidding away under the bed.

My sisters and I froze. If we didn't pick up the guns and put them back in place, we knew we'd be in trouble for knocking them over and for playing in my parents' room. But the rule was we were not to touch Dad's guns. We knew how to handle a rifle, of course. We'd all been taught to shoot at an early age, but handling guns required Dad to be present. We argued and fretted over what to do. We finally decided that calling Mom and asking her advice would be our best chance for survival, so we phoned her at work. Mom instructed us to leave the guns alone, shut the bedroom door, and get our chores done before she got home. Years later, I was still disappointed in myself for being careless around Dad's rifles and wondered why our parents never brought it up again. I'm sure, as I think about it now, they probably had a good laugh at our expense because of how upset we were. Times and kids have changed a lot since those days, and establishing rules is just one of the things necessary when children and firearms share the same house.

Setting the rules regarding guns around children is entirely left to your officer and his or her spouse. Many law enforcement agencies tell their officers how to store their service gun and even provide gun locks. In an officer's home, regarding an officer's children, he will make those rules. As a police mom, your only responsibility is to know and uphold those rules. If you have guns in your own home where grandchildren may have access to them, you need to follow your officer's lead. Consistency is critical for children to know what is expected of them, and there is no wiggle room on gun safety.

The obvious rule regarding guns and children is, of course, that the responsibility is on the adults. Lock your guns and keep them away from the children. That means using a gun safe and/or locks on individual firearms. Some children, depending on age and maturity, may understand the dangers and consequences of touching a gun, as I did as a child, and may be depended on to stick to the rules. But will their friends and cousins have the same restraint? These are questions best left to your officer.

Your officer and his or her spouse will also want to make the decisions regarding teaching their children to shoot or hunt. Many grandparents believe that is a privilege bestowed upon them by tradition, and that may well be the case, but it is your officer who should make that call. There can be severe ramifications for a law enforcement officer who "allows" a child to become injured due to lax safety precautions, in addition to the unthinkable tragedy of a child being injured or killed.

On this topic of guns, I might suggest that if you decide to purchase a handgun for protection or sport, talk to your officer before buying. Decide how and where you will learn to shoot, if you are not already a shooter. Just because a police officer knows how to shoot does not mean he or she should teach you that skill. I recommend taking a class from a qualified instructor. You might want to talk to your officer, however, about what gun might be best for your purpose.

I *do not* recommend allowing your officer or anyone else to choose a gun for you. Your officer may be able to recommend specific guns for their reliability, quality, or other features and possibly point you to a reputable gun shop, but only you can determine which gun is best for you. You will want to handle, and hopefully fire, several guns before purchasing. You'll want to decide what best fits your hand, has a comfortable trigger pull, and can be easily broken down for cleaning. Your officer can advise but cannot decide those things for you. And again, remember to plan for safe storage of any gun you own.

## Other Rules and Guidelines

These are just a few of the topics for which you might want to establish rules and guidelines. Other things to consider might include establishing a place for muddy boots, nasty uniforms, and smelly vests to be deposited when your officer arrives home. You may want to set a rule about where gun cleaning takes place or where a duty belt is stored. Maybe you need a rule about quiet time for your officer to sleep during the day. I'm sure you and your family will have others. The important thing to remember is that these are guidelines that can and will change over time to meet the needs of your family.

# CHAPTER 8

# Supporting Your Officer's Needs

With a handful of ground rules that will ensure that every family member is heard and feels valued, you can begin to determine what each person needs beyond that to adapt and thrive in a police family. Every person will have needs or desires that will make their adjustment to police life easier. Obviously, your officer is at the center of this life change, so let's begin by looking at what he or she may need and what you can do to support those needs.

## WHAT A COP NEEDS MOST

During interviews I did with a group of veteran officers, I asked what they wish their families had known or understood when they first became cops. One response prevailed: "The most important thing a family can do for a new officer is to cut him some slack!" Similar words of advice from these officers were: "Give your officer room to navigate his new life," "Give him time to unwind," "Be accepting of his new role and the characteristics that he develops," and "Be patient and understanding of his moods and exhaustion."

One seasoned veteran said, "The greatest gift a family can

give a new officer is acceptance. That new officer knows he is changing, and he worries about how those changes will affect his family. Patience, understanding, and most of all acceptance will tell that officer he has the support of his family. Nothing means more than that."

Bottom line is that if your officer feels supported at home, all the changes, disruptions, and challenges that arise from having a police officer in the family can be worked out.

## Acceptance and Understanding

Although it may seem that the goal for a police officer should be to not allow the job to change him, that is neither realistic nor desirable. Remember, it is the intense focus and alertness that keep him attuned to danger at work, and it's the rest and recovery afterward that prepare him to go back into that mode for the next shift. Welcome these cycles and their accompanying behaviors. They are what keep him safe; they keep him alive. So the goal is not for him to *avoid* changing but to *manage* the change.

Routines at home may need to adapt and allow your officer to de-stress as he makes the transition to home life. It takes time for his body chemistry to return to a normal state. If problems or questions are thrown at him the minute he walks in the door, you are likely to get a reaction more like one he would use on the job rather than a response fitting that of the loving son, husband, and father the family was hoping to see. Give your officer time to switch back to off-duty mode. If he is new to the job, that switch may take a bit longer, although even after years on the job, the effects of some days may require more time to shake off than others. Try to be understanding of that need. There are few home crises that can't wait an hour or so to be resolved or even be handled by a spouse or parent.

## Barbara

*My friend Barbara arrived home one morning to find her officer sitting in his car in the driveway, not moving, but just sitting there, staring straight ahead. She approached and cautiously knocked on the car window. She could hear the music from the radio blaring. Her son startled at her sudden appearance, then gave her a smile as he rolled down the window.*

*"Are you okay, son?"*

*"Sure, Mom, just chilling before I go inside." He smiled again and rolled the window back up, leaned his head against the seat, and closed his eyes. It was nearly forty-five minutes before he joined his family inside the home, but he was relaxed and cheerful. His time alone listening to his music had done its job.*

Whatever your officer needs to do to let go of the stress and intensity of the job before engaging with his family, try to remember that this is sacred and valuable time. Helping the kids with homework or paying bills does not count. Maybe he listens to music. Perhaps he plays video games, or goes for a run, or does woodworking. He may need ten minutes, or for-ty-five. Allowing him time to change gears is time well spent. It's important, though, that your officer does, after a reason-able period of transition, engage with the family. If he or she is isolating for long periods on a regular basis, there may be cause for concern. You'll find more about that in Chapter 11.

One great suggestion for preserving that decompression time came from a police wife. She often greeted her officer after work by asking how his day had gone and was frustrated when his response was frequently a curt, "Fine." She knew it wasn't always "fine," and she wanted him to talk about things that bothered him. Some days he was open to telling her about calls he'd worked, but other days his unspoken message was a clear, "Leave me alone!" as he retreated to the basement. They developed a code phrase to tell her he needed time to decom-press so not to snap her head off. If he'd had a bad day and didn't want to talk right away, his response to her peppy "How was your day?" was a short but informative, "A lot." She then knew to give him a bit of space. When he was ready, he would share more—or not. But until he brought it up, she left it alone.

## Outside Friendships

In the unique culture of law enforcement, it is easy for an offi-cer to pull away from people who don't understand what his life is now like. He gravitates to a world of cops because he is comfortable with those people. Indeed, friendships with fellow officers are extremely important, and the bond they share is indisputable. Those are the people he can share with and safely unload the weight of a hard day. This is where he feels safe.

Equally important, however, are non-cop friends. Maybe it's a friend from high school or a brother-in-law. Maybe it's the childhood best friend who never believed he would really become a cop. Whoever these friends are, encourage your officer to maintain those friendships. Those are the people who can serve as a trusted listener, a diversion from work, and maybe even be the friend who can best keep your son or daughter grounded.

## Play Time

Hobbies and non-cop activities that they can enjoy both with the family and alone are also important in an officer's life. Whether it's a day fishing, helping a friend with a project, a night of poker, or a day at the zoo with the kids, few things can refresh a person's soul like laughter and fun. Holding onto those parts of himself that have nothing to do with the job will help relieve built-up stress and allow him to be the person you know and love.

## PRACTICAL NEEDS

Acceptance and understanding, of course, do not address all the things that an officer needs. A cop spends many hours a day taking care of the needs of others. It's important for him to know that his needs and comfort matter too. They certainly matter to us, although the needs of our sons and daughters in law enforcement may not be what we expected.

## In The Beginning

Supporting your officer begins even before he or she starts the academy. In fact, it may come as a surprise that you and your family could have an impact on your son or daughter even getting into the academy. Background checks are customarily performed on family members, and most departments conduct at least a cursory interview with the parents and spouse of a new applicant. Some agencies even do home visits and in-person meetings with family members.

All this is, in part, to ascertain whether the recruit will have the support of his or her family. I will assume, though, that if you are reading this, your officer has at least made it as far as the Academy, so we'll focus on the needs from that point on and how you can provide your support.

The truth is many officers do just fine even without encouragement or help from a parent. After all, not all officers have families who agree with their career choice or perhaps the parents are deceased or are not involved. Those men and women still make great law enforcement officers. It is my opinion, though, that every officer deserves the support of his or her family. This is a tough job in so many ways, and a loving family can make the years in law enforcement much easier.

Of course, not every officer wants mom or dad all up in their business. Therefore, I caution you to let your days as a helicopter mom stay well in the past, if you were ever so inclined, and remember that *support* means different things to different people. Let your son or daughter guide your level of involvement and choose what works for both you and them. Check with your officer from time to time to see if his or her needs have changed. The following sections are intended not as instruction but as insight and suggestions.

## In the Academy

Virtually every officer will say his days in the police academy were among the toughest of his career. So much information is thrown at them in such a short period that it can become overwhelming, especially considering their lives or others' may depend on remembering all they are taught. They are learning communication codes; department policies; local, state, and federal law; procedures; driving; firearms; and so much more. All the while, they are being pushed to their highest level of physical fitness. At home, they spend additional hours studying for tests and working out. The bar is high, and they do not want to fall short.

So, what can you do? Give them the gift of time. Keep your demands on their time and energy to a minimum. You might offer to quiz her as she studies for a test, but don't be offended if she declines. Your recruit will have personal study methods and may even have a study group from the academy. Just give her space and encouragement. Many officers struggle through the academy, but it is their classmates who will likely provide the most beneficial encouragement and help. But as in anything your son or daughter has ever struggled with, a mom's belief in their success will matter.

One thing your officer will need during the long days and stressful hours of the academy is good nutrition. You can help by making sure your recruit eats well. A large, healthy meal can be the fuel that gets him through the mental and physical exertion. During his time in the academy, my son calculated that with all the physical training and personal workouts, he was burning nearly six thousand calories a day. It takes a lot of healthy food to fuel the body and brain during these months of training. Recruits who take their lunches each day will need a lot of healthy options, rich in protein and high-carb fruits and vegetables. This need for good nutrition will continue throughout your officer's career as well, so it's a good habit to instill now.

When graduation day finally arrives, make it special. If at all possible, attend the graduation ceremony. It will mean much to your officer to see you there. And doing something to commemorate this occasion will also remind your officer of how far he or she has come. A special dinner with family and friends can be a great way to celebrate.

One of the most frequent questions I've gotten from moms is "What is a good graduation gift for my officer?" Following are a few examples of both practical and meaningful gifts you may not have thought of.

If you come from a law enforcement family as I did, one suggestion may be an item from an earlier generation police officer. A shadow box made up of a father's or grandfather's badge, uniform patch, handcuffs, or other keepsakes makes an inspirational gift.

There are a host of equipment items that may be needed by your officer, including several items that could add a bit of protection to the standard uniform. Does your department approve the use of personal Kevlar vests, like the newer weight-bearing vest that relieves back strain? It is not necessary to spend a lot of money on gifts, however. A pen that writes in the rain, a pocket notebook, an engraved keychain. Knowing your officer is outfitted with all the gear that will allow him to do the job safely and comfortably—*and* remind him of your love—can make a mom feel a little better when he heads out each day. Other suggestions were mentioned in Chapter 6, and I have provided a more comprehensive list in Appendix D.

However you choose to celebrate, include the people that are special to your LEO. Make it a party, and don't forget to take pictures.

## On the Job

Once your officer hits the streets, they will quickly adopt an air of confidence. It may seem that your support is rarely needed.

Of course, there will be times when he discovers a new item of equipment that he sorely needs or he asks for your help in juggling his schedule, but his goal is always to appear to be in full control. He's not, of course, and your presence will be important as he tackles the ups and downs of this life, both on and off duty.

Your officer will have needs to be met during his shift. Maintaining the healthy diet that was started during the academy days can be a real challenge, especially on the night shift. Fast food burgers and fries do not provide the kind of fuel that keeps an officer alert and in top condition. Often an officer can swing by the station to heat a meal in the microwave or sometimes use a microwave in a convenience store in his patrol area, but some days that is not realistic. Providing him with fresh fruit, jerky, or high protein granola will get him through those busy days. It's amazing how something as simple as sending your officer off with an ample healthy meal and snacks can have a huge impact on his ability to do the job well and come home feeling good.

One of your officer's challenges is maintaining balance between work and home. He has a job that makes it difficult to stay in touch with his family during those on-duty hours. It may seem the solution would be phone conversations squeezed in during the quiet moments of a shift. Check with your officer, though, to ensure your calls are not excessive or poorly timed. That can be especially important if he shares a car with a partner and privacy is an issue. Maybe he needs to know that if you are calling during his shift, it really is important and not just a casual chat. Let him know it's okay to tell you that he can't talk. The last thing you want to do is become a distraction from his work. Perhaps a quick text to ask if this is a good time to talk or to request he call you when he has a free minute would be a better way to go.

There are, of course, many other ways we can be there for our officers, meeting their needs for support and assistance. You might offer to bring dinner to your officer while he is on patrol because his regular eight-hour shift turned into a twelve- or sixteen-hour shift. You might deliver rain gear to the police station so he can swing by to get it during an unexpected storm. A police mom who is also grandma can be an important backup plan when a child gets sick at school.

I know more than one grandma who became a full-time caregiver when maternity leave ran out or daycare costs outpaced a police officer's salary. Come to think of it, being a nanny to your grandchildren isn't a bad retirement job when it means you're the one who gets to help raise those precious little ones while Mommy or Daddy are busy saving the world. And through it all, you'll know that in your own way, you are making it possible for your officer to live their dream.

## EMOTIONAL NEEDS

From the time we hold our babies in our arms, a mom is attuned to the needs of that child. It's an innate drive deep within our souls to love and protect that little bundle, even though that little bundle suddenly one day becomes six feet of solid muscle and grit. Our instinct never changes, just our method of showing support. This is something our officers may never understand, even after they themselves become parents. You may expect having children of their own will make a difference, that your son or daughter will see why we still worry and want to protect them, but you could be wrong.

Perhaps they don't think they will feel the same when their child is grown or possibly they believe those protective feelings will disappear. Maybe someday they'll get it, but for now they simply want our love—just not shown *too* overtly. So that leaves us with those same feelings as when they were little children and dependent upon us, but now we are tasked with loving them without embarrassing them, encouraging them without getting in their way, supporting them without being seen. It's a fine line we walk as mothers of superheroes, but we are up to the challenge.

## Being There

This is where I sometimes envy the mothers of daughters in uniform. It seems that our female officers have a greater tendency to talk, to share a bad day, and to relish the comfort and the hug that a mom offers. Our boy-children-turned-cops may struggle to admit a particular call got to them or that for just a quick minute they felt fear. A mom can often tell though, and this is the time when you walk the walk of the promise you made when your officer graduated—the promise to always be there.

Let him know that you are in his corner. Tell him that you have confidence in him and his judgment and abilities. If it would be meaningful to him, remind him that God is watching over him. Tell him you believe he is the right person for the job. He probably knows these things but verbalizing any of them at a moment when his need is greatest can be the emotional support you promised.

Every officer lives with those "what ifs" when a situation does not go well. What if she had said or done something differently? What if she had started CPR sooner or seen the gun in a suspect's waistband? What if she had taken a different route and arrived one minute sooner? They second-guess themselves and tuck those questions away in the back of their minds. Every officer has something they wish they had done differently. Every officer sees and does things that the rest of us cannot fathom.

These are the days a mom's intuitive support means more than ever because they can't tell us why they need that little extra love without explaining the very thing they don't want to talk about. We don't need to ask questions or push them to talk. We only need to be there, loving, believing, and building them up. And if or when they do open up and the words flow, let them talk. Don't rationalize matters or attempt to explain why you think something happened, unless they specifically ask. Just listen. Most often that's all they want. Give them a hug. Prepare a favorite dinner or perhaps suggest a fun outing. This is the kind of support that moms do best.

## SUPPORTING THEIR FELLOW OFFICERS

Remember when your kid was in school, and you were the Class Mom? Your child was embarrassed when you came to her class to bring the lunch that she forgot or to check on how she was feeling. Yet, when there was a class party and you brought the cupcakes, she was excited and happy to see you. This is kind of like the adult version of that.

If there is one truism about police officers, it is that they like food. Maybe it's because so many of their meals are interrupted with a call to roll out or they are so often forced to rely on fast-food joints for sustenance. Whatever the reason, they especially like home-cooked food. So, for Mom—anyone's mom—to show up at the station with homemade brownies or a pot of chili is cause for celebration. And if it's *your* mom, the same kind of accolades received as a kid when Mom brought cupcakes are true again. Suddenly, your officer is everyone's best friend.

Taking food to your son's or daughter's department, precinct, or shift is the easiest way to support the men and women your officer works with each day. It's also the sneakiest way to get to know those who have her back on the job. You might check with the precinct to be sure it's a good day to come by, ask if there are any rules regarding food being brought in, and find out where to park and where to take the food. Be sure to bring whatever supplies will be needed to serve your food as well.

A friend taught me to always bring zip-lock bags and paper products that allow the officers to create a "to-go" bag for snacks to take out on the road. And remember not all officers want to snack on junk food all night. Even when bringing sweet treats or a heavy meal like lasagna, I also bring a good supply of fruit and other healthy alternatives for those who are trying to stay in shape. And don't forget the drinks. On hot summer days, Gatorade is especially welcome.

There are other ways you can support your officer's co-workers too. Stop by during the holidays and offer to decorate the lobby or to clean the kitchen. Most police stations have someone who cleans the offices, but it's likely the refrigerator has not been cleaned in months. Our department, and possibly yours too, has volunteers who spend time at the precinct doing these kinds of things. Ours are called Ambassadors—community volunteers who want to help and support those who protect and serve. They would likely welcome a police mom to the group.

There also may be special programs with which the department will welcome your help and support. Does your local agency have a Neighborhood Watch program in need of volunteer leadership, or do they run a mentoring program for at-risk kids? Keep in mind that every interaction you have with the community on behalf of the department reminds the citizens that police officers are real people, and that they have moms and dads and families who love them. Part of our role is humanizing our officers.

If you have access to a group of children, whether it be your grandkids or a classroom of third graders, encourage them to draw pictures or write letters to their local police officers. Take their works to the precinct and hang them for the officers to see. Write a letter yourself, and sign it as an anonymous citizen, thanking them for the work they do. Encourage your friends to send a note of appreciation or even file a "report" commending a specific officer for a situation handled well. You would be surprised how much those words of appreciation mean to our officers. They are often read at roll call for all to hear.

I came across some inexpensive keychains and dog tags engraved to read "Thank You Officer." I carry them in my car, and whenever I see an officer while on my daily errands, I offer them one of these and let them know they are seen and appreciated. And on that note, this may not be economically feasible for some, but I rarely let officers pay for a meal or coffee when I see them in a restaurant. Even when I told a server that I wanted to pay for the meals of two officers sitting at a nearby table and then watched that table grow to hold six more boys in blue, I figured the tab was well worth the smiles on their faces when the server told them their meal tickets had already been paid. They never knew it was me or that a police mom had taken care of them, just like she would her own son. (Of course, it was a while before I could afford to eat out again, but still...)

There is a saying that one smile or one act of kindness holds the power to turn someone's day or life around. That is never more true than when that simple act is extended to LEOs who see the worst in humanity each day. Whatever you find to do to make any officer smile for just a moment is supporting your child and mine and every other mother's hero-kid.

## TAKING ON THE HATERS

At times we feel a need to show support for law enforcement in general, as it seems the whole world has turned against the police. That's not true, of course, but it may be that those who do hate police officers make the most noise. Anti-police protesters can be loud and, in some cases, have made inroads to tip the scale against law enforcement, but I assure you that these haters are not the majority. Even those who demand defunding the police and push to restrict their authority still call for police protection when they need help. Cities that adopted restrictive policies and cut budgets and personnel have realized they cannot fight crime without the brave men and women who enforce the law. Knowing this, however, does not make it any easier when your officer—or you—are targeted by the haters.

We can't escape the televised images of protestors and rioters throwing hurtful words, bottles, and bricks at officers standing the line to protect people and property. And we hear it from our officers: the restaurant that refused to serve an officer in uniform, the coffee shop employee who wrote "Pig" on his coffee cup instead of using his name, the thug that spit in his face. The hatred sometimes even comes from family members who may have had run-ins with the law.

Fearing we might become a target, many of our officers ask us to remove decals from our private vehicles and avoid wearing our "proud mom of a cop" t-shirts. We hear about the police wife whose car was covered in "kill the cops" graffiti, or the yard sign supporting police officers that was spray painted with obscenities. As a police mom, you will likely encounter some version of anti-police rhetoric. It may even come from your family or friends. Social media can be a hotbed of negativity, with the haters hiding behind their screens with a following of like-minded imbeciles egging them on.

So, how should we react? How can we stand our ground and support our officer without escalating the situation and putting ourselves in danger? Can we make these anti-policers see they are wrong?

As with all stressful situations, the best way to react in the moment is to pause. Take a breath. Look at the situation and think before responding. If you have any chance of controlling the situation, you must first control yourself. And the first decision you must make is to determine whether you need to respond at all.

In that moment, when someone yells out an obscenity against the police in your presence, try not to overreact. Ask yourself if a response is worth it. After all, a person willing to do this is so deeply imbedded in ignorance, you are not going to educate them on the value of law enforcement in a thirty-second parking lot encounter. Let it go. Notice your officer's response. There will likely be none. You may want to follow his lead.

On the other hand, something hurtful said by a friend on Facebook or by good ol' Uncle George at a family gathering can be harder to ignore. Several moms I know have been shocked by a family member voicing the opinion that any cop is a bad cop. Engaging with these clueless people is not likely to change their opinions but, if you do engage, be prepared and thoughtful and know when to walk away.

By being prepared, I mean that you may want to plan what to say in such instances. A great comeback is hard to think of in the moment, but if you plan responses in advance, you will be ready. Then end the conversation. Don't overreact or engage in long arguments; it's just not worth it. Many find the "unfriend" option on Facebook useful. But it is possible to keep your Facebook friends and maintain a relationship with Uncle George if you can agree to disagree. It requires mutual respect and perhaps a bit of love, but it's possible.

Focus on the big picture—the positives. There are far more supporters of police than there are detractors. Ignore the noise from the angry and unaware; hear the silence of the supportive majority. Look for their signs of support. I've started noticing car decals, license plates, flags, jewelry, t-shirts, and signs that tell me there are many citizens who declare their support for our officers. It's inspiring when the cars stopped at an intersection often include at least one with a "support the police" sticker.

What about those times when the "haters" are local politicians or city officials? That's a hard opponent to face, but it may be worth the fight—if you're up to it. Should an issue arise in your community regarding local laws, regulations, or policies, whether for or against the police, there's often a great deal of passion on both sides. My recommendation is to get the facts from a reliable source, which may not be the local media. You want to be informed but not obsess over an issue. If change is needed, keep in mind that change takes time.

In our community, for example, a recent issue was the requirement that officers live within the city limits. Our city has been rated one of the three most violent cities in America year after year. Many officers prefer to live outside the jurisdiction they patrol because...well, who wants to run into the criminal you arrested yesterday while you're at Walmart with your family?

This issue had been on the table for years, with many asking the City Council to remove the residency restriction, believing it would also help retain and recruit more officers. The city council, on the other hand, wanted its employees to live in the community where they work and to pay property taxes to the city that employs them. But officers wanted to have a choice of where they raise their families and wanted their employer (the city) to support them. The arguments on both sides were passionate and loud. Our issue was not resolved until the State Legislature intervened, determining that officers could live anywhere within a two-hour radius of their assigned post.

The issues may be different in your community, but the bickering and tension and even violence are the same everywhere. Whether it's local politics, a police-involved incident gone viral, riots, or something else that has the community stirred up, it is hard to stand by calmly. It's enough to make a police mom crazy.

Try these tips for managing the stress caused by anti-police rhetoric: Use caution on social media. Limit your screen time and scroll past negative posts. NEVER respond. A person this insensitive isn't going to listen, no matter what you say. Instead, remove those so-called "friends" who consistently push your buttons. Make your settings "private" to stop trollers looking for opportunities to argue on social media. You can also change your Facebook settings to allow only "Friends" to comment on your posts and accept "Friend Requests" only from those you actually know. Don't post anything on social media that you don't want people to comment on or respond to in whatever way they feel.

Don't expect friends or family members to understand your desire to defend law enforcement. Surround yourself with those who understand your position—other police moms in your area or even police moms across the country. Try to stay calm, even in the most difficult times. Taking care of yourself mentally and physically will make you feel better and put you in a better place emotionally.

The stress and worry surrounding the negativity in this world, be it from politicians or neighbors, can become overwhelming. If you find yourself bogged down and feeling depressed, it may be time to get professional help. It can be hard living in a society that hates us and our sons and daughters simply because of the uniform they wear. Take care of yourself and support your officer with pride. The haters may be louder, but we are stronger!

# CHAPTER 9

# The Needs of the Family

Everyone will respond to having a cop in the family in their own unique way and, as we covered in Chapter 7 regarding ground rules, their needs should be heard and considered. In this chapter I will talk about specific family members, i.e., spouses, children, and extended family, and what you might do to support them.

## YOUR OFFICER'S SPOUSE

If I haven't said it before, let me do so now: I hit the jackpot in the daughter-in-law department. When my son fell in love, so did I. Of course, she is a cop herself, so there are many differences in how she fills the role of police wife and how a civilian might act in this position. To learn how most wives feel about their role and what needs they have, I did a lot of talking to non-cop police spouses. Later, in Chapter 14, I will speak specifically to police wives. But here we'll talk about police moms and their officers' spouses.

Let's look at police husbands first, because they are, well, easier. It takes a secure, strong man to navigate the role of police husband. Perhaps this is why many policewomen marry another officer. The role can be difficult for someone outside law enforcement due to the demanding schedule, frequent overtime, training requirements, job stress, and all the things that impact any officer. It can be hard to accept the strength, both physical and emotional, that a police officer possesses or the bond she develops with her fellow officers. There are a lot of aspects of being married to a police officer that can threaten a man's ego if he is not confident in his marriage and in his own place in the world. Yet many civilian police husbands support their wives' career and step up to take care of the home and children to a greater degree than their non-police-spouse friends. Others don't.

These men may leave housework or even the needs of the children for their wife to deal with when she gets home. Scenarios like this may benefit from your involvement and support. Start that conversation with your daughter and her husband about what they need. Don't hesitate to ask how you can help. They may appreciate your help with the kids or your offer to provide a meal on occasion. However, I must remind you to make sure your overtures are welcomed.

Police husbands rarely talk about being worried or frightened for their wives on duty. Your daughter's husband would be more likely to shrug it off and express confidence that she can handle anything that comes her way. He may rely strongly on the knowledge that her fellow officers will look out for her. That does not, of course, mean he doesn't worry. He's just not likely to talk about it.

Several husbands I know say they don't allow themselves to

think about their wife being in danger—to do so would drive them crazy. A few I spoke to admit to living in a state of mild denial, not thinking about their wife's job at all. It will do you no good to try to get your son-in-law to talk about such things. You can offer, let him know you are there for him, and then leave it alone. Try to avoid using him as your sounding board as well. Forcing your daughter's husband to think about the risks she faces will do him no good. Stick with the practical things you can do to support your daughter's family. For that, both your daughter and her husband will be grateful.

Police wives are a unique breed. They live a life that few women can pull off and even fewer envy. They are the ones most impacted by this career their husbands have chosen. A police wife must be strong, capable, independent, smart, flexible, creative, under-standing, loving, supportive, and—oh, did I mention, strong? If she is not all those things in the beginning, she will likely grow into the job. But possibly not.

There is a reason police officers get divorced at a rate well above the national average. It's a life that is tough on a marriage. If it is to succeed—and a huge percentage of police marriages do—a police wife has needs of her own that she, her officer, and her family, including her mother-in-law (that would be you), will need to support.

A police wife will feel every step of the journey into police family life. And the journey can be made more challenging if she married this man before he became an LEO. Tracey, a police-wife friend, shared her experience with me over an afternoon of wine and donuts. (Don't judge!)

Tracey said, "I married an engineer. He worked eight to five, Monday through Friday, with four weeks of vacation every year. We had plenty of money and a secure future. We started a family believing we'd have the perfect life. Then, wham! In a matter of months, all that was gone. My engineer husband quit his six-figure job and accepted a position in another state as a police recruit. He'd always said he wanted to be a police officer, but I never thought he would actually go through with it.

"We had to live on our savings for six months while he was in the academy, and following his graduation he had an income one-third of his previous salary. The baby and I moved to his new city where I knew no one. I had to go to work, leaving our one-year-old in daycare. I ate dinner alone every night and went to bed alone. My husband became someone I didn't even know, which didn't matter because I rarely saw him anyway. Our baby girl barely knew her daddy. I wanted my original husband back and our original life. We were all miserable, all three of us, and I didn't know what to do."

Knowing she is now a happy, supportive police wife, I asked my friend what changed for her. "I met other police wives. And police moms," she added, giving me a wink.

I'd first met Tracey at one of our New Police Family Orientation events held for family members of Memphis officers. Even though her husband had been on the department for almost two years, she'd asked to attend, saying she was hoping for a new start on this life so she could try to save her marriage.

Tracey's story illustrates that need for support. Whether she married an engineer or a police officer, a police wife need not go it alone. She needs friends who understand her crazy life. She needs a family who shares her pride and accepts the challenges of having an officer in the family. She needs an officer-husband who works with her to establish solid communication, workable routines, shared home responsibilities, and compassion and understanding for each of their emotional needs. And she may well need a mother-in-law who shares her concerns, supports her efforts, and surrounds her with love.

Your daughter-in-law will want to understand the needs of her officer too. Invite her to go along to any Family Orientation or gatherings that your officer's department may offer and encourage her to join any wives groups in the department or local area. These provide the best way to meet other police wives who may become her longtime friends and supporters. There are several books I recommend for police wives as well. You'll find those listed in Appendix C. Books make a great gift for a police wife upon her officer's graduation and any time thereafter.

Moms, remember that your daughter-in-law is riding a wave of change as she and your officer transition to a cop family. She is on the front line, watching the mood swings, exhaustion, and personality changes, often not understanding most of what she sees. She may at times feel overwhelmed, saddened, confused, and resentful. More responsibility will fall on her shoulders with her husband not home to help with household chores or caring for the children. She is learning to balance her own emotions of pride, fear, confusion, isolation, and frustration. I hope you already have the kind of relationship with your daughter-in-law that allows you to offer her the compassion, love, and support she needs. Remember, it is you, more than anyone, who shares her worries for her officer's safety. It is you who can understand her mixture of pride and frustration, fear and dedication.

It may take effort and compromise to build a good solid relationship with your police-wife daughter-in-law. But remember, you are not in competition with your officer's wife. I know it sometimes may feel that way, when you are both wanting time with him on his only day off or you feel shut out because he shares things with her that he used to share with you. But love is not a competition. You both love the same man and ultimately want the same thing: his happiness and wellbeing. Your daughter-in-law is your partner in loving and caring for your son. If you accept and respect the person your son chose to share his life, care for her well-being, and honor the union they share, you will likely be a welcome expansion of their family and a valued supporter of their police life.

## FAMILY DRAMA

Early in my involvement with police families, I was surprised and more than a little concerned when several police wives I'd grown close to talked about the mothers of their officers in a very negative way. It seemed as if their lives consisted of constant battles between police mom and wife. I couldn't imagine how either wife or mom could manage this life without the support of the other.

Whether you love your daughter-in-law (or son-in-law) like your own child or have a strained or even non-existent relationship, your officer has chosen to go through life alongside this person and she or he is a part of your Police Family. Let me first address those moms who are shut out either by your choice or your in-law's, or those who can barely be in a room with the person your son or daughter married without sparks flying and tears flowing. I am talking primarily about the moms of married sons here, because it seems only two women who love the same man can conjure this kind of drama.

## When the In-law Relationship is Strained

If you haven't already, you will soon learn that as we get older we often value peace above righteousness. As the matriarch of your officer's family, it is up to you to set the tone. It doesn't matter what your daughter-in-law said or did, it falls to you to create peace within your family. Do this for your grandchildren (current or future), your extended family, yourself and, most importantly, your officer. It may not be possible to become best friends with your daughter-in-law and may not even be possible to have a civil conversation, but you can create peace.

I have seen drama in police families, but however miserable a wife may choose to make herself and others, she cannot disturb your peace unless you let her. There are, of course, exceptions, so please forgive me if this advice cannot be applied in your relationship. I am in no way judging or pretending to know what will work in every situation. These words of advice I have learned from other moms who have been in those circumstances and found some resolution and improvement over time.

My harsher self wants to say you should put on your big-girl panties and just make it work. My compassionate self knows you've been wearing your big-girl panties since the day you met her, and it's not that easy. But, as the more experienced grownup and the mother of this amazing young man who is your officer, you may have to be the one to guide the relationship with his wife. If you want calm, you have to *be* calm. And in her defense, she is the wife of a police officer, and I firmly believe that this may well be the second hardest job on the planet. (I consider his to be the hardest.)

I have included a chapter for police wives in this book, but if you truly want to try and understand what it's like to be a police wife, I highly recommend you read the book *I Love a Cop*, by Ellen Kirschman, Ph.D. And after you read it, pass it along to your daughter-in-law with a nice note telling her you understand a little better now. And for fun, read and pass along a copy of *Bullets in The Washing Machine*, by Melissa Littles. Both of these books will give you great insight into her life.

You might begin by examining your role in the relationship. Are there things you may be doing that in your mind seem completely innocent and normal but could possibly create friction or make her life more difficult? Of course you mean no harm, but your daughter-in-law does not come from the same set of life experiences as you and may have her own history that tells her otherwise. Are you, inadvertently, sending her a message that she is not valued or not good enough for your son?

Did you exclude her in some way? Have you been critical of her parenting or housekeeping? Whatever you may have done, if it is an ongoing habit, stop it. Accept her and make sure she feels it. Tell her that you love your son and accept that he has chosen her as his life partner. Apologize to her for whatever you have done that made her feel unaccepted and ask for her forgiveness. Then forgive yourself, whether she does or not, and move on.

I would suggest that after reaching out to your daughter-in-law and apologizing for whatever you may have done (specific or nonspecific), that should be the last time you bring it up. Don't keep asking what you did wrong or begging for forgiveness. Just be nice from that point forward. It goes without saying that you too will need to forgive, even if you don't know exactly what it is you are forgiving her for.

If the relationship is so damaged or the distance so great that you cannot visit together, mail (yes, snail mail) a birthday card, a "Thinking of You Today" card, or a note of appreciation now and then. Make sure Christmas cards and Valentine's cards are addressed to both your son and his wife. Give individual Christmas gifts to each of them. Send her a gift card for a massage or pedicure, something that will pamper her a bit. Post a picture of their family, including her, on your Facebook page. And never, ever say anything against her to your son or anyone else in the family.

If your son and his wife live close by, be especially careful of intruding on their limited time together. You may have to stand in line for your son's attention, but that does not mean you have to forgo your relationship with him. Invite the two of them to dinner or on an outing where everyone has something to do other than sit in awkward silence. A trip to the zoo or the theater or a group activity with other family members are all good ideas. And when you are with your grandchildren, be sure to compliment their mother to them. (Come on, you can surely comment on what a good job Mommy did picking out their outfits for the day or what pretty eyes they have, just like Mommy's.) Anything you say will get back to her, so make it something positive.

Give it some time, and allow her some time, and with consistent warm and friendly behavior on your part, things will likely improve. Be patient. Just keep being the loving mom you've always been, but now you include her in that circle of love, even if it hurts a little at first. Your son will love you for it, and even the worst daughter-in-law can't fault you for your efforts, as long as you are sincere and don't overwhelm her with your overtures. The end result is so worth it.

## When the Love is Shared

If you already have a loving relationship with your daughter-in-law or son-in-law, your support for their role as an LEO spouse can be especially valuable. You are in a position to offer practical assistance and emotional support, and you are likely to receive the same in return. The key to providing help that is welcomed is to listen. I once heard a wise woman say a mother-in-law should never give advice unless it is requested, and then she should only give half as much advice as she thinks is needed.

When your son-in-law talks about a weekend project he is tackling or a fishing trip he wants to take while his officer wife is working, offer to keep the kids. When your daughter-in-law is exhausted and would give anything to sleep late, hear her cry for help and ask for the kids to spend the weekend with you. Don't wait for them to ask before offering your help. Just assume your officer and his or her spouse are tired, stressed, and stretched to their limit. They may not ask because they don't want to impose, but they may welcome a mom's caring hand. Just be sure to be respectful of what they consider helpful.

Other than caring for the children, how can you provide support for your officer's spouse? That may depend in part on how new the spouse is to the law enforcement family and the community in which your officer lives and works.

A new wife (or wife of a new officer) has much to learn and will likely be juggling an array of feelings about her role. She is learning, just as you are, how this job will impact her officer and their lives together. You can help her learn and understand by sharing resources, like this and other books mentioned previously, and encouraging her to make connections within the Blue Line Family.

Most communities have some sort of group for police wives, be it official through the department or an informal Facebook group. Sadly, some groups are not particularly supportive and are sometimes more gossip fests than informative or helpful. Be aware that negativity exists and encourage your daughter-in-law to look elsewhere if necessary. There are many positive, informative, and supportive police wives groups, and she will hopefully find one in her community. One good place to start is with the National Police Wives Association. They have state chapters across the country.

Perhaps most important, though, is to let your daughter-in-law or son-in-law know that you are there for them. Whenever you are worried about your officer because of an incident he or she may be working, know that your officer's spouse is also worried. You will both find it easier to weather these tense times *together*. Be strong for your daughter-in-law. Let her know she can lean on you. You'll likely find that it works both ways as she becomes a source of comfort for you as well.

## YOUR OFFICER'S CHILDREN

While the adults in the family are figuring out what they need to make police life work for them, someone needs to listen to the children as well. Of course, they may not be able to put their needs in words or even identify what it is they want, but it's important to hear what they are saying, both verbally and nonverbally. The adults in the family will want to stay attuned to the moods and behaviors of the children and listen for clues that they may have needs regarding their new life as a cop's kid.

Of course, it will be mom and dad who have both the responsibility and privilege of being there for their children most of the time, so be sure to talk with your officer and his wife about their beliefs and desires concerning their children and the job of law enforcement. You don't want to cross any lines with what you say or explain to the kids. But it is true that children are often more comfortable asking the hard questions of their grandparents rather than Mom or Dad. Kids often see grandparents as the rock of the family and there are times when Grandma's loving reassurance is the best medicine for a child's worries.

Children are experts at covering their emotions, often in an effort to avoid worrying their parents. A grandmother may be the person they confide in or with whom they feel most comfortable letting their guard down. You, of course, will want to let their parents know of any serious concerns that arise, but there is much you can do to comfort your little ones and help them adjust to their role in a police family.

When a child seems worried that their officer parent could be hurt or killed on the job—a fear they may not want to share with their parent—you can respond in your own soft and gentle way to provide comfort. Make sure your grandchildren know they will always be loved and always have you, a parent, or someone they can talk to about their worries. Let them know that grownups sometimes worry too and that it helps to share those thoughts. Reassure your grandchildren that they will always be cared for and loved.

You cannot make promises that you someday may not be able to keep, such as promising that Daddy or Mommy will always be safe or will always make it home. But you can reassure your grandchildren that their police mom or dad is very, very good at their job and that they have lots of other police officers nearby to help. Most importantly, they need to know that Mommy or Daddy loves them so much that they will do absolutely everything within their power to always come home to their children.

If your grandchildren are worried about the negative statements they hear from TV or outsiders regarding law enforcement, there is much you can do to show them how wrong those sources may be. With your officer's approval, you can tell her about the things Daddy or Mommy does to help people and point out what officers are doing when you see them on the job. When my grandkids were younger and out with me, I would go out of my way to thank officers we saw and buy their lunch if we were dining. That gave me the opportunity to talk about why people should be grateful for the things the police do for us. From there, it was an easy step to include the fact that, because not everyone knows or remembers all the good things our officers do, some people don't like the police. For young children, that's all they need to understand about society's negativity.

For older children, you can go a bit further and talk about incidents that have turned some people against the police. Even then, I like to come back to the fact that those people are not seeing the whole picture and are judging all officers by the actions of one or two and ignoring the many positive things our officers do. Your willingness to talk about society's perceptions of law enforcement in a way that explains but does not frighten your grandchildren will assure them they can trust you with their thoughts and concerns.

It is human nature to fear most what we don't understand and that is especially true for children. Teaching children what a police officer's job really entails is important in their ability to fit into the life of a police family. And since children are naturally drawn to those real-life heroes who are our police officers, firefighters, soldiers, and other first responders, it is easy to teach even little ones about their parent's job. But as the child grows and matures, their ability to understand the job increases and the information you offer to them should increase as well. Encourage your officer to let them visit the precinct where mom or dad works. Give them opportunities to meet their officer's partners and fellow officers. Include the children in department Family Days where they will see other officers and families. These events mean more than you might imagine in helping a cop's kid understand they too are part of a police family.

When I was a kid, Memphis held an annual Police Picnic in July. Hundreds of police families would gather to share tables upon tables of potluck dishes and hamburgers straight off the grill. There was entertainment, games, contests, and demonstrations by the K-9 and Mounted Patrol units. I made friends there whom I saw only once or twice a year, but those friends were important in my life. They reassured me that my way of life was normal, and these people were part of my police family. To this day, I recall their faces and the bond we shared. I don't remember their names, or maybe never knew them, in that way children have of making friends but never feeling the need to learn one another's names. What I remember was that I felt a part of something big, something special, something I could count on.

Another way of making a child feel like they are part of this extended police family is to include them from a young age in making and delivering treats to a parent's unit or precinct. My granddaughter loves it when we bake cookies or deliver a meal to her officer mom or dad at work. She will talk all morning while we bake, about police officers and her desire to become an officer herself one day. (For a while it was a toss-up between becoming a police officer or Wonder Woman, but following in Mom's path won out, at least for the time being.) I always clear it with her mom or dad before showing up, but we then "surprise" the whole shift with lunch or goodie bags. My sweet granddaughter beams with pride at being showered with the attention and gratitude of all the officers, and she gets to share a rare lunch with her mom or dad. Sitting in Mom's police car or watching Dad with a class of recruits teaches her more about their jobs with every visit, which in turn lessens her worries.

The goal, of course, is to make sure your grandchildren feel safe and to instill in them the sense of pride that you carry. You already know what a comfort it is to focus on the pride and other positive aspects of the job. Share that with your grandchildren and show them the joy of being part of a police family.

## EXTENDED FAMILY

Families. They can be great, and they can be genuine stressors. Most families have members that cover the spectrum. I have sisters who are incredibly supportive of my officer son and his officer wife. They are almost as proud of them as I am. But even my sisters will never understand the fear I carry deep down inside for my officers' safety. We can't expect them to understand what it's like to be a cop's mom. This is a life that no one outside the Thin Blue Line can truly understand. Still, they can be supportive, and I hope your extended family is so inclined.

In the real world, however, not all family members are supportive of our police officers. Some have had a bad experience with a cop in the past. Yes, they probably brought that on themselves by failing to cooperate in some way, or possibly even crossed the line of the law, and now blame the officers involved for their bad experience. It's also possible they encountered an officer on a bad day or even had a run-in with an officer who really should not be on the job. Perhaps that negative family member follows a particular political/social belief that cops are generally bad people.

Whatever their reasoning, it can be hard on you and your officer to have a relative who dislikes the police in general, particularly if they are vocal about their feelings. But there are some things you can do to minimize their negativity, or at least avoid hearing it. After all, that person's opinion is not relevant. It serves no purpose to listen to their rantings.

If that anti-police relative is someone close to you and you want to preserve the relationship, it will help to find one common point you can agree on. Maybe it is a mutual understanding that the world would be in chaos without law enforcement officers. Or, possibly, an agreement that not all officers are "bad" and that there are officers who treat people fairly and try to help those in need. It may be that you can only agree that you both love and care about the safety of your officer. Whatever the common point is, establish a place where you can agree and then leave the discussion there. You can even ask that person not to discuss their negative opinions around you. You can agree to disagree.

That family member who refuses to come to an agreement regarding police officers in general, or even just your officer, may need to be handled differently. It is okay to "unfriend" that person on social media. It's even okay to walk out of the room when he or she starts spouting negative comments about police officers. You are under no obligation to listen to someone, even a relative, speak poorly about your son or daughter, their career, their department, or their blue sisters and brothers. What you want to avoid is any confrontation with this person. You won't change their mind and they won't change yours, so it's best for everyone if you don't engage in the conflict.

A good friend whose son is an officer in another state says that half her family is anti-police. Whenever the family gathers, usually for holidays or special occasions when everyone is supposed to be celebrating, certain family members will intentionally start arguments with her or her son about police actions. She says it is very hard to listen to cousins she has known all her life make assertions that her son and all officers are bullies, crooks, and worse. For years, she would argue with them, defending her officer and offering proof that most police officers were good and honest, and for years, she would leave these family gatherings filled with stress and anger.

Finally, her son convinced her to ignore the comments and not respond to whatever they said. By the second year of family gatherings, after she took her son's advice, the ugly comments and accusations stopped. She avoids these family members as much as possible and focuses her time on others whom she enjoys. She admitted that she occasionally overhears them say something negative, but by walking away, she can enjoy her family gatherings again.

Hopefully, however, those negative types will be rare or non-existent in your family. There will be others, fortunately, who are extremely supportive. The next generation of family members—those nieces and nephews and young cousins—most likely look up to and admire your officer son or daughter. Your grandchildren, both from your LEO and your civilian adult children, will enjoy hearing a few stories of the calls your officer takes that have a positive outcome. Let them relish the "superpowers" of your real-life hero. To see your officer in uniform is quite a treat for young family members, and it may have a positive influence on their views of police officers as they grow up.

The adjustment to police family life is not likely to be entirely smooth for everyone. This job changes routines, schedules, habits, feelings, and people. But slowly and surely, adjust we will, as we come to understand ourselves, our officers, and our families perhaps better than we ever have. By listening and discovering each person's needs and working to meet those needs wherever possible, we will become stronger.

# CHAPTER 10

# What a Police Mom Needs

We have talked a lot about other people's needs and how to identify and meet those needs. But what about you? After all, this book is for you. You have feelings and emotions that run the gamut, and you may not yet be sure how to control or get comfortable with them. After all these years as a police mom, I still wish I knew how to rein in some of mine. But I have found a few tricks that help.

The first step in coping with police life is to define what it is you are feeling, what brings on those feelings, and what you and others can do to keep your emotions on the positive side of the equation. You might start by making a list showing all the various things you feel about your life as a police mom. Be honest with yourself; no one else will see your list, so put it all out there. We all have mixed feelings about this life; include the good and the bad.

You may discover needs you don't know how to meet or can't control on your own. You may need things from others and not know how to get them to provide for you. Don't let that stop you as you write your list. You first have to know what it is you feel and what you need before you can think about putting those things in place.

Once you have listed all your feelings under either "Positives" or "Negatives," go back and add what triggers each one. Now you can formulate a game plan to address each of the items on your list. For example, on the "Positives" side of my chart, I might list Pride. Under Pride, I would list, among other things, that it is triggered by seeing my son in uniform. (Even after fourteen years, that can bring tears to my eyes.) I would also say it is brought on by hearing other officers and commanders talk about good things my son has done or hearing about calls that challenged him but turned out well. From that awareness, I can conclude that I need those rare but precious opportunities to see my son dressed in uniform and opportunities to talk with his supervisors and fellow officers.

To meet those needs, I may need to ask my son to stop by on his way to work occasionally or I might time my visit to his precinct just before he goes into roll call. Doing those things remind me of that wonderful feeling of pride, and help bring on the feeling of confidence that comes with it.

Similarly, on the "Negatives" side of my chart I might list Worry. It is triggered by his working in a dangerous part of town and by the fact that I don't really know what he does during an average shift. As I examine ways I could reduce the worry from these specific triggers, I come up with several ideas. I can avoid social media reports of the fights and shootings in this area, which are largely exaggerated anyway, and I can learn more about my son's job. The goal, of course, is to identify what we can do to increase the emotions shown on the "Positives" side of our chart and decrease the unpleasant emotions listed under the "Negatives."

As a side note, I am often asked, "Do the worry and fear ever go away?" Those feelings will ease over time, but to be honest, no, they don't ever go away completely. These are our sons and daughters working the streets of America, and there is danger there. The concern for their safety is real and constant. There will be times when your community is relatively calm and your worries will decrease, but there will also be times of unrest—riots, political activities, an officer-involved shooting, or accusations of police brutality. These are the times your worry-meter goes sky-high and fear takes hold.

To completely stop worrying about your officer may feel like you would have to stop caring about him or her. Of course, that's not going to happen. Your goal, instead, is to manage your fears and calm your concerns so they don't interfere with your life or your officer's. That is a realistic and attainable goal, and you can learn to do that in a very short time. It's a matter of identifying your genuine needs and putting specific actions and thoughts in place. You can do this!

## DEFINING YOUR NEEDS

We are likely to discover that we have more control over our emotions than we realize. We can do things to bring on those positive feelings and suppress the fear or negative emotions. We do not have to become victims of our emotions. Even more important is that we not allow ourselves to become victims of our son's or daughter's chosen career. It is not their doing that brings on our worry. And in most cases, it is not their responsibility to relieve our worry. Moms, we must own our emotions and our reactions. You'll be surprised how much power you have to control those things.

I already gave an example of a positive emotion—Pride—and what I could do to bring on that feeling more frequently. So, now let's look at an example of what the "Negatives" side of your chart might look like. Let's start with Worry, since I used that as a short example earlier. That is likely high on your list, with perhaps a dozen things listed below defining the causes. A typical list might look something like this:

| Emotion: Worry | |
| --- | --- |
| **Triggers:** | My officer looks tired and seems stressed, even on his days off. |
| | He works a lot of overtime and I never know when I can stop worrying. |
| | I'm not sure backup will be there when he needs it. |
| | It seems like everyone hates the police. |
| | I don't know much about real police work. |
| | I feel alone, like no one understands me. |
| **My Plan:** | I will offer to keep the grandkids on the weekend so he can relax. |
| | I will ask my officer to text me when he gets off duty. |
| | I will visit his precinct so I can meet his fellow officers. |
| | I will avoid social media sites that spread negativity about police. |
| | I will learn more about the job and ask to do a ride-along. |
| | I will meet other police moms who can guide and support me. |

By identifying the various triggers for our emotions, we can examine what things might be within our power to mitigate negative feelings. In this example, some of my solutions may depend on my officer's cooperation, and some are things I cannot change, but I can control my reaction to them. I can't change the fact that so many people seem to be anti-police. But I can reduce my exposure to news and social media spouting negativity. And I can ask my officer to text me at the end of his shift so I know he is safe for one more day.

I can meet his fellow officers so I will know who will be there when backup is needed. I can request to do a ride-along so I can see what working as a police officer is like. And I can find a group for police moms, either on social media or an in-person group that gets together to support one another. This last item is a biggie.

Just having people who understand our feelings and this life will go a long way in relieving fear and concerns. Other police moms can let us know what behaviors are normal, suggest solutions for our concerns, laugh with us when something is funny but also scary, and hold us up when we can't stand alone anymore. Having a group of fellow police moms—sisters, as it were—can be the best support for just about any challenge or feeling you may be having.

Even if some things you identify as your needs require help from your officer, such as a text message or an okay to visit the precinct, be aware that this is not the same as making your officer responsible for your feelings. Whatever ways we find to put our minds at rest, that is *our* task. As parents, we must realize that this is the career our sons and daughters have chosen, and they have worked hard and sacrificed a lot to get there. Our officers are highly trained professionals, and they are prepared to do their jobs well. Our job is to support them and let them know we believe in them. Our job is to tell them we are proud of them.

Find a way to rein in your worries and fear and other negative feelings so your officer doesn't know they exist. You will still worry. At certain times, you will still face near crippling fear. But you will know how to control those emotions and understand that you can feel fear yet still be supportive and confident in your officer.

## ASKING FOR WHAT YOU NEED

Once you have a list of the specific things you need from others, you are ready to solicit their help. Keep in mind that you have already identified several ways to control your worries or other feelings all on your own. You are in control! It's okay to ask others to assist you. You may even want to tell your officer, daughter- or son-in-law or others what you have done for yourself before asking for their support. Doing so will likely make you feel less needy, and perhaps even come across to that person as such. You will be reinforcing the fact that you are a strong woman asking for assistance. So, what might you ask of your officer?

## What you Need From Your Officer

Using my previous example of working to control my worry, I will have a conversation with my officer to ask for what I need from him. I will first pick the right time for that conversation: not when he is exhausted and wants to sleep, and not when I can tell he is closed off after a tough shift. I might pick the second day of his weekend, whatever day that may be, so he'll be more relaxed. I might plan this conversation over lunch or while we are doing some activity together. I'm going to begin by telling my officer how worried I *was* (past tense!) when he first started his career and how I have met other police moms and read books that have helped me learn to relax a bit. Then I will ask for the few things I still need from him.

I will explain that I still have trouble sleeping at night until I know he is off duty and out of harm's way, and ask, "Would you be willing to send me a text each night to let me know your shift has ended? Or give me a quick call? I'm always available to you if you want to talk, but all I need is a short text to say you are off duty now." Then I might say, "I hear a lot of police moms have done ride-alongs. I'd love to do that. Can I go out with you or should I request a ride-along with another officer? Would you tell me how to get permission and schedule a ride-along with your department?" Note that some departments have a policy against ride-alongs with a family member, and some officers and family members worry that riding with their own officer may pose a distraction should a situation become dangerous. Hence, a ride-along with a different officer may be the way to go. I might conclude our conversation by saying that he has seemed tired or stressed lately, so would it be helpful if I took the kids the next weekend so he could sleep or do something fun? By ending the conversation with things you would like to do for him, it's likely the conversation will end on a positive note for both of you.

## From Your Officer's Spouse

My list of feelings and needs, as well as those of many police moms I know, includes loneliness. We often don't see our LEO kids as much as we used to, and we miss them. Perhaps they work in a different city or are just busy and tired, but we can be left feeling abandoned. Asking your officer for more of his time is often not going to solve the problem, especially if he is already feeling stretched to the limit. Maybe your daughter-in-law is the better person to help with these feelings. After all, it is often the spouse who controls much of your officer's off-duty schedule.

Tell her how you feel without sounding whiny or demanding. Recognize that she too may feel shortchanged on her time with her officer. Ask her how she's doing. Let her know that you'd like to help her too. Offering to help with the kids can bring a lot of joy and fulfillment to your life and ease her daily burden as well.

Spending time with your daughter-in-law can also ease your feelings of loneliness and be much more informative than time with your officer would be. She may share details of their activities, plans, and even job-related stories much more readily. Take her to lunch or take her shopping. Embrace your officer's spouse like you would your officer and you both win.

Sadly, however, not every family shares the kind of relationship that provides for that positive time together. You may find yourself in competition with your daughter-in-law for your son's time or you could encounter a degree of hostility if you ask for her support. Know that to your officer, his marriage and his wife will come first. That's as it should be. So avoid confrontation and never push your officer to choose between his mother and his wife. The loser in that contest will be your son, and there will be no winner.

If your relationship with your daughter-in-law is not good, you'll want to limit your exposure to a toxic situation and try your best to be respectful and supportive of her needs. It may well be that she feels threatened by you, afraid she will not measure up. Or she may be so unhappy herself that she needs more support than you do. Either way, kindness is the best option. As my mother always said, "Take the high road. The view is better from there."

For some odd reason, it took me a while to realize that one solution to my wanting more time with my officer son was to invite him and his wife to come to dinner. Simple as that. Most wives would welcome a night of not having to prepare dinner (or breakfast or lunch or whatever meal your officer is available for) and husbands usually go along with any plans their wives make, so invite them over or out to eat. Keep it casual and fun, and you'll likely get repeat visits.

## From Your Officer's Department

It might surprise you to know that your officer's department cares about the needs of family members and many of them offer information and programs to help meet those needs. If information has not been shared with you already about the types of support the department offers, don't hesitate to call and ask. Starting with the academy days, many departments offer programs where family members are invited to the facility for a tour, orientation, and an opportunity to meet commanders and trainers. They supply information on everything from what to expect from police family life to how to get help for a variety of issues.

Some departments may link you to support organizations in your community. Others hold annual Family Day events where spouses, parents, and children are invited to attend presentations by various police units, participate in games and activities, and socialize with other police families. Your officer may or may not have received information about these activities, so be sure to ask and, if they don't know, call the department to inquire.

Most departments offer counseling services through Employee Assistance Programs, and many provide services to immediate family members as well. We will address that topic in more detail in a later chapter.

Some departments, usually through their academy, provide or recommend specific reading material to help family members understand the world of law enforcement and how it may impact families. Your officer's supervisors or commanders may know if those are available or make other recommendations.

Another great source of information your department may provide is a Citizen's Police Academy. This is a weekly class, usually spread over six to eight weeks and held at your local police precinct. It is normally open to any citizen interested in learning about the role and workings of the police department. Most departments utilize guest presenters from their various units to instruct and demonstrate what they do to keep their community safe. Although not specifically for police families, these programs provide a wealth of information and bring a much greater understanding of the work our officers perform.

When I went through our local Citizens Police Academy, I honestly didn't expect to learn much, since I'd been around the MPD all my life. I was amazed at how wrong that assumption was. I learned a great deal, met many great officers and community supporters of our police department, and had a lot of fun. Some of these citizen academies offer opportunities to handle and use police equipment and shoot firearms at the police range. In most instances, pre-registration and background clearance are required to attend these programs, so I recommend checking what your local requirements are, if this is offered in your community.

Some law enforcement agencies welcome the support of citizen volunteers through an Ambassador or Volunteer Program. These are everyday citizens who help and support a specific precinct in myriad ways. They may decorate the lobby for the holidays, collect donations of teddy bears for officers to carry in their cars for children in distress, bring in meals for officers on special occasions, or offer their support in any number of ways. Being involved in your officer's precinct as a volunteer, a regular Ambassador, or just a mom bringing goodies on occasion, is a great way to get to know the men and women your officer works with. You may also gain an understanding of their work environment.

If you don't live close to your officer's precinct or if she prefers that mom not hang around her "office," volunteer at a different location. You will learn a lot, even if it's not the specific place your officer works.

If on your list of needs for this police mom life is a desire for a ride-along or tour of a specific unit, you will need permission from the department. That may be something your officer wants to arrange herself or it may be up to you to make those arrangements. Don't be afraid to call and ask or even stop by the desk at your precinct. For years, I have called or stopped by my local precinct so often (it also happened to be where my daughter-in-law worked until a recent reassignment) that the desk officers came to know me as "Momma Carol." They knew that, like every good mom, I would take care of them with baked goods or lunch and always lots of hugs.

Just a reminder, when calling your local law enforcement agency, be sure to avoid calling their emergency number. Every department has a non-emergency line that you want to use for general inquiries.

## SUPPORT FOR AND FROM OTHER LEO MOMS

You are not alone. That's really the whole point behind this book. Going back hundreds, if not thousands of years, the mothers of brave peacekeepers have watched their sons and daughters go off to protect their communities. I imagine we are not unlike those mothers of ancient times in our worry and pride. In more modern eras, I can assure you that what a mom in Indiana feels about her child's job and safety is very much the same as the mom in California or New Hampshire or communities the world over. The strength and wisdom we acquire over time become lifelines for the next ones who inherit this role. All we have to do to ease their fears is reach out.

In our local moms group, we have mothers of officers with twenty-five-plus years on the job and moms whose sons and daughters graduated the training academy only weeks ago. When I was first forming our MPD Moms group, I was told by some of our more experienced moms, "I don't need the support of a moms group. I've been doing this a long time, and I've made it this far without anyone's help." But when I asked how they felt in those first few years, making it through the tough times without anyone's help, they remembered the struggle and tears.

It doesn't matter whether you are the mom trying to figure out this new police mom life or if you are the mom who has survived the hardest days, you can find purpose in a connection with other police moms. An experienced mom can be that strength and comfort that the new mom seeks.

Over the years, I have discovered several regional and national groups for LEO parents—moms in particular. I have joined several of these, while a few others I decided were not for me. Don't be discouraged if the first group you join does not offer the kind of support you are searching for. Check out a few others. There are dozens to choose from, and each has its own personality, generally matching that of the group administrators.

As I mentioned in the previous chapter regarding police wives groups, some moms groups also quickly deteriorate into gossip, whining, or political and social tirades. A few are oriented toward fundraising for injured officers or surviving families or even for each other. Several are designed specifically as prayer groups, while a few are primarily memorial pages for officers lost in the line of duty.

I encourage you to find something that serves your needs—a group that empowers and strengthens, a group that comforts and supports one another. Those groups are out there, and you should not settle for less. My personal favorite is Moms of Police Officers (MOPO). Wherever you go, find a place that matches your philosophy and reflects the role you want to have in giving and receiving support as an LEO mom. I have listed a few of the national organizations in Appendix C, but keep in mind that social media is ever evolving, so a quick search on your platform of choice will turn up others.

Most police mom groups that I have seen are set as "private" groups on social media. That's important if you want to talk openly. The best social media groups have a strong vetting system in place to ensure those joining the group are indeed who they say they are. Each group administrator may have a different way of ensuring their group is secure and private, with varying degrees of strictness, but the goal is the same—your safety and that of your officer.

Most groups also have rules in place to which members are required to adhere. Again, there are varying degrees of strictness, but the goal is to keep the experience of participation enjoyable and comfortable for all. If you apply to one of these groups, understand that you'll likely be asked for certain information to help them verify that you are who you say you are and that you will be a good fit for their group.

If you find there is no local group of LEO moms in your area, consider starting one. It is truly an easy thing to do because so many of us want and need a connection with other police moms. It's not necessary, however, to have a formal group of moms in order to support one another. You just have to make a connection. You can ask your officer if his colleagues and partners have mothers in the area that you might connect with. You can try volunteering at precinct activities in hopes of meeting other moms. And you might want to introduce yourself to those who appear to be police moms when you attend Family

Days or other department events.

I got quite a surprise, however, when I introduced myself to a woman at a department event who seemed to be about my age. I thought she was likely a police mom, proudly watching her officer marching in an honor guard. I was shocked when she told me she was the officer's grandmother. I realized that as my son has been on the department for a number of years now and I have aged right along with him, police moms are getting younger every year. Still, this is a sisterhood that spans age, location, and all else. All that matters is that we share the pride, concerns, and way of life of an LEO mom. So, whether your "moms group" is two people or two hundred, you don't need to walk this road alone. And don't let another mom be left alone on that road either. We need one another. We are stronger together.

## How I Found Other Police Moms

For the first few years my son was an officer, I did not know a single other police mom and, for the most part, I managed just fine. Then, one July day, we had an officer shot and killed after responding to a domestic violence call at a downtown hotel. He wasn't even officially yet on duty but was on his way to work when he heard the call on his radio. He responded to help his fellow officers. I attended the officer's funeral, alone, and began wondering if this tragic event made other mothers worry too.

The next year another officer was killed while serving a warrant. My worries grew as the reality set in that my son was placing his life on the line every day. I realized my family and coworkers did not understand why these deaths made me worry so. Neither had occurred in the area where my son worked so, as sad as they were, what did they have to do with me? I began to wonder if anyone could understand how I experienced these events or how frightening they were to a cop's mom.

Over the next few years, through involvement in local government issues, I came to know many people within the police department and many wives of police officers. But even their emotions were not the same as mine. Where were the other police moms? Would they understand? I had no way to know, because as involved as I'd been with our local first responders and their families, I still had not met other law enforcement mothers.

With yet another officer's death on August 1, 2015, this one seeming even closer to home, I could no longer do this police mom thing alone. I posted a message on several Facebook group pages to which I belonged, all designed to support our local police and fire departments: "Looking for moms of Memphis Police Officers interested in connecting as a group. Contact me." Within hours I was hearing from other moms, and within one week we had dozens of Memphis police moms anxious to find someone who would understand how they felt.

MPD Moms was formed. Since November of 2015, this amazing group of women has come together both online and in person to share stories, worries, laughter, and love. We've grown to include hundreds of moms spread all over the world, whose lives intersect simply because our children are Memphis Police Officers. We come from all backgrounds and live our lives quite differently, yet we are friends. We are family. We are sisters bound by the Thin Blue Line.

Finding or, in my case, founding a network of police moms has changed my life in more ways than I could have imagined. Each of us has discovered a safe harbor where we are understood and accepted, supported and embraced. We have all commented on how surprised we were to find so much in common. I remind my fellow moms frequently that although our lives may be filled with differences, we all raised superheroes and that takes a special kind of mom.

One of the most comforting aspects of belonging to an LEO moms group is how safe we feel there. Because we all are in the same boat, so to speak, we have similar concerns for privacy and confidentiality. We are each concerned for our officer's safety and our own. We are worried about our officer's mental and psychological well-being, watchful of anyone or any situation that threatens our officer's job or reputation. Security is paramount in our group.

In this group, we can say things to each other that we would never share with outsiders. We respect each mom's feelings, even when they may differ from our own. We allow one another to be a little crazy, each in our own way. Whatever question one of us may have, we can ask, knowing there's no need to feel embarrassed. Whatever need one of us has, there are sisters who will provide. No judgment, no drama, just support.

# CHAPTER 11

# When The Going Gets Tough

We worry enough about our officers on an average day, but there can come those occasions when our officer is in trouble. That trouble may come in various forms—an injury, an accusation of unnecessary force, a shooting, or any incident that brings emotional distress. All a mother wants to do is fix it so her son or daughter is all right. But this law enforcement world in which they live may limit our ability to fix it. We are not, however, powerless. A mother's love and support are never more important than when her officer is facing mental, emotional, or physical pain.

In law enforcement there are many ways in which a situation, a career, or a life can quickly become very difficult. Our officers are trained to deal with many of these; however, some circumstances are unimagined or else training for them is impossible. Yet here we are, facing the unimaginable. Over the next few pages we are going to look at many of the most spirit-breaking situations we and our officers may face. But first, some thoughts on how to deal with any challenging situation. What we do in those times can go a long way toward comforting our officer or, conversely, inflating his anguish. Think carefully before responding to be sure to convey the message you want your officer to hear.

## YOUR NEXT STEP MATTERS

The call comes when you least expect it—in the middle of the night, or while you're enjoying lunch with a friend, or during a work meeting. "Mom, I'm going to be okay, but..." Or "Mom. It's bad." Or worst of all, "Is this Mrs. Smith? Are you Officer Billy Smith's mother? I'm afraid I have bad news." It may even come as a knock on the door. Two uniformed officers stand waiting.

When the proverbial shit hits the fan, if your first reaction is to panic, STOP! There will be time and opportunity to fall apart later. Now, while your son or daughter is suffering, is not that time. Whatever the news, start with three deep breaths. Remind yourself of all those times when your child was little and needed you—a broken arm, skinned knee, playground bully, or a broken heart—you went into *"Mom Mode"* and dealt with the situation. The stakes may be higher now, but you can do this. You can be what your son or daughter needs in this moment. Remind yourself too that there is support for you out there. You are not alone.

You—and your officer—will need to distinguish between what you can control and what you cannot. That's critical, no matter the situation. For example, you can control *your own* thoughts, beliefs, behaviors, emotions, words, and actions. You cannot control other people, events that have already occurred, politicians and their yammering for attention, the actions of department leadership, the media, criminals, department regulations, current laws, or public opinion. To be sure, what you do and say can and will *influence* some of those things you cannot control, but people will do what they do and your task is to control yourself.

Be sure to *Respond*, not *React*. A reaction is immediate, emotional, and often intense. It can also miss its target, be easily misunderstood, and even be hurtful when the intent was just the opposite. A response, however, is thoughtful and deliberate, and is much more likely to convey the message you want to send. So, whether it is in response to the initial news of a bad situation, a later visit with your officer, a statement to the media, or a conversation with the command staff, take those deep breaths, and let your words be thoughtful, your actions calm, and your focus on supporting your officer.

Whatever the circumstances you face, you will do well to take a step back to get clarity and perspective. Look at the big picture. Think long term. What is the objective? What outcome do you and your officer want to see from this? It is certainly easy to get buried in the minutiae and drama, but an occasional step back to remind yourself where you are going will help you stay focused on the things that matter. The rest will work itself out.

As details of an event emerge, you may hear many versions of an incident. As a mom you are searching for answers, so it's easy to assume those things you hear are true, but that may not be the case. There's a reason a law enforcement agency will refuse to make public comments about an incident right away. The truth is not always immediately apparent. Be patient.

Consider the source of what you hear and don't rely on gossip, media, or public opinion. Investigations take time and information emerges slowly. Limit your exposure to social media or TV news. Keep an eye on your grandchildren too, and you may want to keep them away from social media for a while. Limit what you and your family share with others.

Some of the serious circumstances our officers may face take time to play out. Whether it's recovering from an injury or facing a legal battle or emotional crisis, it may take weeks, months, or even years to reach a resolution. Patience will be needed, as well as a long-term plan.

Maintain those activities that allow you to relax and replenish your soul. Exercise, meditation, a walk in the woods, even a brief break from the moment or a series of deep cleansing breaths will help you get through a day. Stay in touch with your friends who are supportive and comforting. Even better are those friends with whom you can both laugh and cry. Seek out those people who understand your challenges; often that will mean those other law enforcement families who have survived similar events.

One word of caution here: If you are privy to confidential information, do not under any circumstances share that with anyone, even your closest friend. To do so may severely impact you and your officer in a negative way. To ward off questions, no matter how innocuous they may seem, it's probably best to develop some canned responses ahead of time, along with apologies for not saying more.

If you reach a time when you become overly distraught or anxious, please don't hesitate to get professional help. There are counselors who are familiar with the things LEOs and their families face and who are trained in supporting you through tough times.

As parents, we want to be the rock our officer can depend on, to be strong and reliable, comforting and protective. The simple truth is we cannot be those things if we fail to first care for ourselves. One way to do that is to start preparing now. Learn what resources are available for times of crisis. Find out what procedures your officer's department uses in an emergency. Build a network of Blue Sisters—those fellow LEO moms who will understand your fears and share their strength with you.

One final word on coping with crisis. Early in this book, I mentioned that you may want to rely on prayer to ease your worries. Never is this more true than when your officer is facing a serious challenge. It matters not what your beliefs may be or what religion, if any, you adhere to. It doesn't even matter whether you have lost your faith, are not close to God, or have never whispered a prayer in your life. There comes a time when circumstances are beyond our control and we will do anything to help our son or daughter. That's the time when a prayer may be the only answer. It may be that a prayer spoken in earnest with a heart full of love for your family will bring hope, strength, and peace to even the toughest of times.

## THE THINGS WE FEAR THE MOST

These next few sections will be some of the toughest you will read within the covers of this book. But let's face it, these are the things we most need to talk about—the things we fear the most, or should. So buckle up! We're going to go through this together, just like we will for this whole journey.

I call them the "Big Three"—the three most common worries of a new police mom. Actually, the new police mom may at first experience only two of these fears, until she learns how devastating the third can be. Those two most recognizable would be the possibility of our officer getting seriously injured on the job or losing their life in the line of duty. The one you may not have considered is his having to shoot another person. All three of these events can be life altering for all involved, but let's look at each one separately.

### On-the-Job Injuries

There are many ways an officer can get hurt on the job. Consider some of the more common risks: fights, falls, dog bites, needle pricks, cuts, and car accidents (both minor and serious). Add in the possibility of being hit by a vehicle, stabbed, and shot, and we suddenly realize how dangerous it is out there for our officers.

I've taken several phone calls from moms who just faced one of their worst nightmares. Her officer is in the hospital, having survived a serious and tragic injury. His future at that point is unknown and possibly dependent on a series of surgeries and weeks or months of rehabilitation. She is both devastated and grateful because despite his injuries, her child is alive. That fact never escapes a mom as she sits by her officer's bedside.

We all wonder how we will be notified if our son or daughter is seriously hurt while on duty. I can assure you, if the call comes from your officer, you have likely already won the lottery. If your officer is able to make that call, you can breathe easier. If your officer is so seriously injured that she cannot call you herself, you will likely get a phone call from a lieutenant or captain, or possibly a knock on the door from an officer ready to escort you to the hospital to be with your son or daughter.

Keep in mind that it is usually the next of kin who is notified first, and your married officer most likely has listed his or her spouse as next of kin. Depending on the severity of your officer's injury, the department may or may not notify you as well. You may want to have a conversation with your son- or daughter-in-law about notifying you when an injury occurs. Having a plan in advance will help put you at ease.

You can expect a large presence of fellow officers at the hospital, especially immediately following the incident. The Chief or Department Head will reach out to you soon, if not the moment you arrive at the hospital. You will likely be contacted by a Union representative as well. It may be this representative or your Chief of Police and their assistant who will answer all your questions as information becomes available.

This is also a time when you will see the full strength of the Thin Blue Line in action. Police wives and moms, often with surprising speed, organize to offer an array of assistance for your family. From standing with you in the early hours at the hospital to creating a meal delivery brigade, caring for children, running errands, or even organizing fundraising activities for your officer, your police family will be there for you.

Depending on the nature and severity of your officer's injuries, as healing continues it is customary for him or her to be allowed to return to light duty—working a desk, taking reports, or some other job away from the streets—as soon as possible. Light duty may be frustrating for your officer because they're anxious to get back on patrol; however, it is usually the best option. It keeps them somewhat active within their law enforcement community while in recovery mode.

Your biggest challenge as your officer recovers may be to avoid becoming overly protective. I can tell you, that's hard. It's easy to feel like the universe has now proved we have cause to worry and we don't want our son or daughter to return to such dangerous work. You may want to turn to your fellow police moms to help you through this, remembering, just as in the beginning of your officer's career, you have to allow them to follow the path they are meant for. Let your pride show and your worries remain hidden, as you encourage your officer in her recovery and return to duty.

## Officer-Involved Shootings

If you are fairly new to police life, you may not be aware of the damage an officer-involved shooting can cause to a career or an officer's mental health. But let's put it in perspective. Only 27% of police officers ever fire their weapon in the line of duty. Most, in fact, never even draw their gun. Shooting a suspect is never the goal. There are times, however, when someone's life is endangered and it becomes necessary. The residual effect of an officer using deadly force depends upon several factors.

The most important factor is whether the wounded person lives or dies. That outcome impacts more than that one life. Another consideration is who was shot. Was it a confirmed suspect? If an officer shot a known criminal who was actively attacking that officer, other officers on scene, or innocent victims, there may be less public reaction. It gets much more complicated when an officer fires at a minor or an individual with a clean record, even if that person was armed or noncompliant. That does not mean to imply the shooting was not necessary—just that it is more likely to be questioned. Other influencing factors might be whether or not other officers saw the threat and fired also. Was there body cam footage showing the incident? Did the shooting victim have a weapon? Did the officer identify himself as such? The list goes on.

All of this is to say, every situation is different and therefore cannot be detailed here in a few short paragraphs. Even a totally justified shooting, one leaving few questions for investigators and deemed to be the reasonable and necessary response to the situation, can have a profound effect on the officer and his career.

Most of our sons and daughters have never shot at or killed another human being and may be very troubled when they are forced to do so. It can be a heavy burden to carry, regardless of how necessary it may have been. An officer in this situation will be debriefed and offered counseling by his department, but that may not be enough. Even former military soldiers who have seen battle and killed in warfare may experience this shooting differently. It will, in all likelihood, seem a much more up-close and personal experience and can leave even a military veteran severely shaken.

In many communities, every fatal or high-profile officer-involved shooting is investigated by a State Bureau of Investigations. This is to reduce and hopefully eliminate the possibility of a biased investigation. Many people do not believe a department can fairly investigate one of its own. There will be citizens—including the family of the suspect—who claim the shooting was an act of unnecessary and unlawful force. There will be claims of innocence on the part of the suspect and declarations by family members that their baby is innocent of whatever led to the shooting. We often see huge outcries on the part of some citizens and media who actually know few details of the incident. Absolutely nothing an officer ever does in their career will generate a more emotional response.

Investigations take time, however, and there is little to do but wait. That in itself can take a toll on the officer, his blue brothers and sisters, and definitely his family. The waiting can be all the more difficult given some of the department's standard but necessary actions involving your officer.

You can expect that as quickly as the "shots fired" call goes out, many additional officers will arrive on the scene, including supervisors and commanders. Those arriving first will ensure your officer is safe and check the condition of the suspect. They will provide first aid as needed until emergency medical personnel arrive. A supervisor will take the officer's gun, remove him from the scene, and separate any other officers that may have been involved. It is often these two actions that most disturb the officer, leaving him feeling as if he is being judged and accused of wrongdoing by his own people.

That is not the case and, if necessary, you should remind him of this. The gun is taken for ballistics testing to confirm the officer's involvement and the cause of death (if applicable) of the suspect. Officers involved in the incident are separated so that investigators can conduct a preliminary interview with each person without accusations that stories were concocted or collaborated. Sometimes it can take a while for those interviews to take place, so an officer's isolation can be longer than seems reasonable or, at times, it can lead to the officer being allowed to go home before being given the chance to tell his side of the story.

Actions taken may vary not only by department but by incident. The intent is to allow for a thorough and clean investigation with the objective of showing the truth surrounding any officer-involved shooting. The officer can expect to be relieved of duty or moved to desk duty for the duration of the investigation. Some departments will issue the officer a replacement gun right away, while others have a policy of not doing so until the investigation ends.

There are times when an investigation does not provide definitive answers, and a final report submitted to the presiding District Attorney (DA) leaves room for doubt as to the justification of the shooting. The decision to file charges against an officer lies with the DA, with or without a Grand Jury ruling. The power held by the DA should not be underestimated; however, theirs is not the only power in play. Right or wrong, our society has come to wield substantial power.

Not long before I started our local MPD Moms group, an officer-involved shooting occurred in our city. An officer just three years on the job had placed a young man in the back of his police car while waiting for details on the man's outstanding felony warrants. He then proceeded to take the suspect out of the back seat with the intent of handcuffing him and making the arrest. The suspect had other ideas and attacked the officer with the handcuffs, beating him severely while attempting to take the officer's gun. The officer fought for his life, knowing that he would be a dead man if the suspect got his gun. Eventually, as the struggle continued with the officer on the ground and being strangled, he was able to get control of his gun and fire, killing the suspect before help arrived.

The DA recommended the officer be charged with voluntary manslaughter, but the Grand Jury failed to indict. A State review of the shooting determined there was insufficient evidence to support charges against the officer. The public outcry led by friends and family of the suspect, along with negative media coverage that began immediately after the incident, did not let up. Civil charges against the officer filed by the suspect's family kept the case in the spotlight for years, even following multiple dismissals. It seemed the public would not let it go and was determined to punish this officer.

The officer and his family were moved to an undisclosed location for their own safety. Eventually, the officer was forced to resign from his job, move out of state along with his parents, and live for years with the mental and emotional anguish caused by not only the shooting but also by the vicious hatred and accusations of the community.

I suppose the good news is that now, years later, he has built a new life, has a family of his own, and has found happiness. This brave officer and his family did not deserve any of what happened to them. This officer's mom showed herself to be one of the strongest mothers I have ever known, as she stood by her son's side through the nightmare of this police-involved shooting. Sadly, across the country, their experience is not unique.

## Line of Duty Deaths

Our ultimate fear. We don't often speak of it; we dare not acknowledge it. But underlying every worry and concern we have, there is this—our son or daughter could die doing this job. I will tell you that I am one of those people who believe they can handle anything, as long as they know what is coming. Even in the face of something as huge and horrific as suddenly losing a child, I want to know what will come next. What should I expect? Not all of us think like that. If you are not ready to let this thought enter your consciousness, that's okay. Skip to the next section and come back to this when you are feeling stronger—or don't. Reading this will not change the outcome. If, however, you are like me and prefer to prepare in advance, read on.

There is nothing I can write here that will make it better or easier if your officer loses his or her life. You know it, and I know it. But what I can tell you is you are not alone and you will never be forgotten or left behind by your department or the Thin Blue Line family. We call them Angel Moms, those moms who have given the ultimate sacrifice of a child in the protection of their community.

*There is no stronger person on earth than the mother who has buried her child and goes on breathing.*

— ANONYMOUS

As each of us wrestles with this, the greatest of our worries, there are a few things I will share. Store this information in the back of your mind, in that corner where you hide this particular fear, and hope, as we all do, that we never have to think about it again. But first I will try to answer a few of the questions about what to expect should the worst ever occur.

For a very long time, I thought I was alone in wondering about this, wanting to ask but afraid it would sound inappropriate. I knew, in the end, it wouldn't matter. But I wanted to know how I would be notified in the event my son was killed while on duty. I pictured it being like the movies, with a mother being notified of her soldier's death—an official car arriving with an officer and a chaplain to share the tragic news. But then I wondered, would they take time to find a chaplain and officer in full dress blues to notify a parent that their son or daughter may have just taken their final breaths? In most cases, the reality is a bit less dramatic and a lot more practical.

Often, two or more officers, one possibly a chaplain and the other a member of the command staff, will come to your door—assuming, of course, you're listed as the next of kin. If not, that visit will be to his or her spouse. A second team may come to you also or you may have to depend on the spouse to initiate that notification. Smaller communities may, out of necessity, simplify the process even further with a single officer coming to your home or workplace. However, the fastest and most commonly used form of notification is a phone call, usually from your officer's colonel or chief. The call may be immediately followed by an officer arriving to escort you to the hospital to be with your officer.

You might want to ask your officer how notifications are handled where he works. Of course, if that is not in the same town in which you reside, the notification will most likely come by phone, although some departments will request your local department send someone to notify you in person.

Funerals for fallen officers are another topic many of us wonder about. You may have seen the elaborate services—the pomp and circumstance, honor guards, bagpipes, and huge numbers of people at the funerals for officers lost in the line of duty—and wondered who puts all that together. And who pays for it? And are you required to do all that?

To answer the last question first, no. Some departments or unions have officers put their preferences in writing. If not, you or your officer's spouse have the choice regarding a traditional police funeral. Honestly, however, it would be rare for that not to be chosen. As with any death, the decisions regarding funeral arrangements are left to the immediate family. That said, your officer's department is also a family and they are likely devastated by your son's or daughter's death as well. The department will want to honor your officer with long-held traditions. You, or your officer's spouse, will have discretion and options regarding arrangements, but the department will want to hold a ceremonial farewell for him.

In most cases the department, or possibly the union, will

make the arrangements and advise and assist you with many of the details. They can obtain a church that will accommodate a large number of people. They will post an honor guard with your officer before, during, and after the wake and funeral service. They will provide speakers, with your approval, from the department and help you with any others you wish to add. Their intent is to honor your officer and take as much of the burden off you as possible. But the department will also respect your wishes and integrate your ideas for the service and burial into the final plans.

One of the arrangements the department will likely make is a Sea of Blue. This beautiful display of respect and honor brings a procession of police and other law enforcement agencies together to drive a designated route with blue lights shining so the entire community can come out to watch this final farewell. A Sea of Blue is one of the most heart-wrenching and inspiring sights to see.

Oftentimes this parade of lights will contain hundreds of cars from law enforcement agencies across the region. I have stood along the highway to watch far too many of these tributes to a fallen officer and even ridden in a squad car in a Sea of Blue. Tears have been shed from both positions, as not only my pride but also my awareness of how fragile my son's life truly is has been renewed.

Expenses for this funeral are, for the most part, the responsibility of the department or city where your officer worked. Often the family has the option to request additional services from the funeral home that may not be included in what is already covered.

After all the ceremonial farewells have ended and life moves on, there may come the question of a memorial in honor of your officer. I've heard of many types of memorials, from highway signs to marble statues, depending on the department's budget and protocol. Your officer will also be added to the National Police Officer Memorial Wall in Washington, DC. You and your family will be invited to attend the ceremony that honors all fallen officers which is held during National Police Week in May of each year.

## THE THINGS WE DON'T KNOW TO FEAR

While many of us spend time worrying about the "Big Three," it may not occur to us that the most common threats our officers face are internal. This job can take a tremendous mental, emotional, and psychological toll on those within the ranks of law enforcement. I saw evidence of this just a couple of years ago.

### Sharon

*The call came at about 10:00 p.m. (that's 2200, in law enforcement time). Sharon, one of the moms in our local group, was clearly distraught.*

*"Carol," she cried, in a pitch well above normal human sounds. "I need your help! My son, Seth, called me twice tonight*

saying he couldn't do this. When I asked what he meant, he started crying and said, 'Everything! This job! This life!' Carol, I'm afraid he might hurt himself!"

"I'm glad you thought to call me," I responded. "Now, Sharon, stop for a minute and take a breath. I need to be able to hear your words. Take a couple more nice deep breaths and tell me what's going on. Where is your son now? Is he safe right now?"

Sharon assured me her son had calmed down, seemingly crying himself out, and was with his wife and safe for the time being. I asked, "Did something happen to trigger his thoughts tonight? Or do you think this is something that has been building up in him? Let's think about what might be going on."

Through a long conversation with Sharon that night, I heard her breathing slow down and her voice return to normal as we talked about her son's eighteen months on the job. Seth had graduated top of his class and immediately been assigned to one of the busiest precincts in the city. He'd done well on the job, even been awarded a Life-Saving Medal in his first year for rescuing two children from a burning car. His family was proud, especially his little girl, who was just four years old. She understood her daddy was a hero. Seth continued to shine on the job and had recently been nominated for Officer of the Month, based partially on his role in busting a child-trafficking ring, even though he insisted his role in that case was minimal.

Of late, however, he'd been moody and a bit unpredictable, snapping at his wife before work and retreating to his game *room as soon as he returned home. But those moods never lasted more than a day or even a few hours before he'd be back to his normal self, laughing with his wife or playing make-believe with his daughter. No one had seen any real cause for concern until this day when he broke down. Sharon didn't know what to do or how to help her son or his family. She was worried and felt helpless. She told me that now as she thought back, there had been subtle changes in her son of late. He didn't even seem happy about the awards he'd received.*

## Psychological and Emotional Damage

For every mom who wonders why her son or daughter has changed so much since becoming an officer, look no further than this section right here. Sure, all the things we talked about earlier like the demands of the job, the schedule changes, and the exhaustion are contributing causes, but when those changes you see are more profound—deeper, troubling, and life-changing—you may find your answer within the next few pages.

We all go into this role as a police mom with worries about our officer's physical well-being. Will he get injured in a shooting, a fight, or an auto accident? Could he be killed while on the job? It's true, there are enough ways our sons and daughters can be physically injured or even suffer loss of life to keep us wringing our hands for decades. The most common injury sustained by an officer, however, is not physical but psychological. I am reminded of an adage I first heard in relation to soldiers in the military, but it is all too true for law enforcement officers as well.

*There is no such thing as an unwounded warrior.*
— ANONYMOUS

Since most LEOs begin their careers as patrol officers, they are likely to encounter things on the street no man or woman should ever have to face. The sights, sounds, smells, and experiences they face can be overwhelming on any given call, but as the months and years go on, the cumulative effect can be tremendous. Whether it be a single incident or a slower build-up over a long period of time, the effects are often damaging. The human psyche of modern times is not conditioned for the horrors that a bad day on the job can bring to a police officer.

Our kids most certainly were not raised to take these things in stride, and all the training in the world will not change that. Usually, they are able to adapt, compartmentalize, put up walls, and even joke their way past the horrific suicides, mass murders, abused children, tragic accidents, rotting bodies, gruesome injuries, and death notifications. But too often there is nowhere for all those memories to go except deep inside.

The same can be true of the pain and frustration they feel due to the all too frequent hatred directed at them from the public. They face name calling, false accusations, threats, and danger both real and perceived for themselves and their families. How do they continue to do their jobs in the face of all this? They shove it inside, put on the mask of indifference, and get back to work.

Seth's difficulties came with that first heroic act of saving those two children. The medal they pinned on his uniform only served to remind him of the terrible burns on one child's body, and of the third child, an infant, whom he had not been able to save. He thought of those children every time he kissed his daughter goodnight and each time he helped her dress for pre-school. Every touch of her soft, silk-like skin reminded him of the young girl from the burning car who would never again have skin that smooth. Even eight months later, he could not clear his mind of the steam rising from her body or her screams as he'd lifted her from the car.

Seth had not been completely open about his role in capturing the child sex traffickers either. He'd been involved enough in the case to have transported one of the perpetrators to jail, the whole time wishing he could pull his cruiser behind a building and dole his own form of justice to this piece of scum. What if his daughter had been victimized by these evildoers? And there were other cases too: the domestic violence case just the previous week where the seven-year-old little boy had been hurt trying to protect his mother, and the twelve-year-old runaway he and his partner found living in a culvert.

Seth was not suicidal—not that he hadn't thought about it—but he was considering leaving the career he'd dreamed of all his life. But that's not what he wanted. He just wanted to stop seeing the hurt and frightened children in his sleep and wondering if he was good enough for the job—good enough to protect them all. That's what he shared with his mom and dad after he'd been in counseling for a few weeks.

His wife had ultimately insisted he get help, and he didn't want to let her down. It had taken a couple of false starts, however, to find a counselor he felt comfortable with. But now he had someone he could turn to whenever the job crept up on him and wouldn't let go. And because Seth had learned ways to cope, his mother now felt she too could manage her fears with a little help from her police mom friends.

## PTSD / PTSI

You might know it as PTSD (Post-Traumatic Stress Disorder) and assume it affects only soldiers in battle or victims of violent crime. I would say you are wrong on both counts. Some of the most respected professionals in the field believe it is not, in fact, a disorder but rather an injury, thus labeling it as PTSI. Others prefer the label of PTSS (Post-Traumatic Stress Syndrome) or just Post-Traumatic Stress (PTS), believing that the symptoms of this condition are normal and expected reactions of mentally healthy humans to horrific experiences. I tend to agree with these experts and typically use the terms PTSI or PTS.

Ellen Kirschman, Ph.D., known as the Cop Doc, explains it well. "People struggle long term with disorders, they recover from injuries." Whatever it's called, it is a serious, potentially disabling condition that is treatable and recoverable.

We think of Post-Traumatic Stress most often in relation to the battlefield or perhaps pertaining to the victim of a violent crime such as rape or beating—a trauma caused by a single incident or experience. Certainly, our officers face situations capable of being so traumatizing they can lead to this diagnosis. Being shot in the line of duty or seeing a partner killed come to mind as events that can cause PTSI. But there is another form of this condition, one brought on by an accumulation of smaller, less traumatic events occurring over months or years, called Cumulative Post-Traumatic Stress Injury.

Critical incident stress, that which is caused by a single event, is easier to recognize and treat. The symptoms usually become evident within a very short time and may last anywhere from a few days to a few months or years. Any first responder on the job for any length of time has likely experienced one or more of these traumatic events. A small percentage of them will develop PTSI as a result.

Cumulative traumatic stress, however, is the gradual build-up of horrifying or heartbreaking moments, scenes that cannot be forgotten, mistakes made, and feelings of helplessness, shame, or regret that an officer doesn't talk about. This buildup can damage one's physical and mental health. We saw a lot of this type of PTSI in health care workers over the years of the COVID-19 pandemic, and it develops similarly every day in the lives of officers who are overwhelmed by non-stop violence, crimes against children, and lack of department or community support.

PTSI, in either form, can be debilitating and life-changing

and can even become life threatening. Signs of PTSI may be obvious to the alert eye but can be easily overlooked by the uninitiated. Symptoms may be denied or explained away by an officer unwilling to admit what is happening to him. These signs of trauma include physical symptoms such as headaches, indigestion or stomach upset, chest pain, increased blood pressure, and unexplained medical problems.

Other symptoms may include withdrawal from social interaction, mood swings, trouble sleeping, repeated nightmares, changes in appetite, use of alcohol or drugs, loss of concentration, or difficulty in making decisions. More serious signs may include unexplainable anger, violent outbursts, aggression, irritability, depression, excessive guilt, flashbacks, confusion about where he is and what is happening, or a preoccupation with a triggering incident and a desire for retaliation or a chance to go back and do things differently.

It's important to realize that what is traumatic for one officer may not be for another. Many factors influence how an officer will respond to an event or series of events, including his background, previous trauma, psychological makeup, and other stressors in his life. There are also some things that can help protect an officer from PTS. Having a department and supervisors who are competent and intuitive of officers' needs, peer support programs, family support, and positive role models who demonstrate resilience are among these.

An officer who has the ability to manage his emotions and distance himself from situations, along with good problem-solving skills, will likely handle stress better. It is important that an officer be able to remain optimistic and have confidence in himself and his decisions. None of these factors is a guarantee, however. The unexpected nature of a traumatic event can knock down even the strongest among our heroes.

Cops don't like to think of themselves as victims. They see themselves not as someone who needs help but as someone who *gives* help. The notion that they need help goes against the higher standards to which they hold themselves. Although most departments offer some form of help to officers, that help may be refused or be inadequate to allow that officer a smooth recovery.

It can be devastating to watch your son or daughter spiral out of control in a fight against PTSI, especially if your officer is rejecting the idea of professional help. But we don't have to sit idly by. If your officer has not returned to normal, or almost normal, behavior within three or four weeks following a traumatic incident, it may be time to step in.

If your officer is extremely moody or showing signs of aggression, let him know that violence in any form will not be tolerated. Make clear what is acceptable behavior but be sure to do so without demonstrating aggression on your part. Present your concerns and state your opinions calmly and confidently. Provide reassurance that he can cope and that his feelings are normal. If you can get your officer to talk about the incident, listen without judgment and allow him to express his feelings of anger, grief, and self-doubt. Remember, an officer's need to talk or not will vary with the individual and the situation. Your goal is to give him a safe space to talk, if he will. Focus on problem solving, not assessing blame. Express commitment and love—let him know you will always be at his side, that you are there to support and help.

As moms who love these injured officers, we are subject to similar associative trauma as we watch our officers struggle. Take care of yourself too. Understand that you cannot "fix" your traumatized officer or the situation; we can only comfort. Find support for yourself, someone to talk to. It's critical that we seek professional help also, especially if we may be the only one close enough at that moment to offer help to our officers. It may be that a professional counselor could guide you in assisting your officer as well.

## Suicide

"Why would a cop commit suicide?" a friend asked. "I mean, don't they know what that does to those left behind? They see it all the time, so why would they do that to their families?"

The truth is there are as many reasons as there are suicides, and there are a lot. Between January and July of 2022, there were already eighty-two suicides by law enforcement officers in the United States. In 2021, there were one hundred and fifty police suicides, and in 2020, there were one hundred and seventy-four. But 2019 brought the highest rate in the past decade with two hundred and twenty-eight suicides. Cops are two to three times more likely to kill themselves than to be killed.

These deaths could be attributed to the stress of the job, family troubles, a lifelong struggle with depression, or any number of things, but it is my assertion that every police suicide is a line-of-duty death. In a job that aggressively pits society against our officers and then makes it painfully difficult for an officer to seek help for mental health issues, the job cannot help but contribute to an officer's suicide. Sadly, there are few, if any, law enforcement agency Benefits Departments that agree with me.

Over the years that I've been leading the MPD Moms and MPD Family groups, I've received several phone calls from police moms (and one from a police wife) telling me they were afraid their officer may harm himself. In every call, the fear in their voices was the same and it sent the same chill through my heart. For me, the distress of suicide is greater than any other form of death caused by this job because I know that not only did that officer lose his life, but he had been hurting for a good while preceding his death. I'm glad to say that not one of those officers I received calls about carried out their inclinations to end their lives, but we will never know what might have happened if mom and others had not been vigilant. Never, ever hesitate to intervene, to speak up, and to insist your officer seek help.

The stigma of suicide must end. If as a society we cannot talk about suicide, we cannot hope to treat its causes or help its potential victims. It's akin to—in fact, it's a continuation of—the old refusal to talk about depression or post-traumatic stress. Slowly, society and many law enforcement leaders have

learned the importance of open communication on these matters and are encouraging their officers to seek help. We must
do the same within our families and social circles.

So, what are the warning signs your officer may be at risk
of suicide? Some of the common things to watch for include
substance abuse, serious prolonged depression, a marked change
in personality, unusually reckless behavior, a previous suicide
threat or attempt, giving away personal possessions, a recent
significant loss in his or her life, or a pending anniversary of a
significant loss. The hardest reality, however, is that there are
not always signs or indications an officer is troubled. Remember,
they are trained to not show emotion. We have to look beyond
what they want us to see. Still, much of what goes on in our
officers' minds will remain beyond our ability to recognize.

If you do pick up on signs that your officer may be thinking of ending his life, don't just worry in silence—speak up!
Be assertive and express your concern. Don't avoid the word
"suicide" by asking benignly, "Are you okay?" It's all right to
ask directly, "Are you thinking about harming yourself?" or "I
need to know, are you thinking about killing yourself?" Tell
your son or daughter you are worried and do not want to lose
them. Remind them of the people who will be affected by their
actions. Ask them to get help and tell them that seeking help
is a sign of strength.

Before you go into this conversation with your at-risk officer, plan what you will say. Prepare your case and be ready to
explain what behaviors you've seen that make you concerned

for his safety. Do not make light of the situation or joke about suicide, even though that may seem like an easier way to bring up the topic. He needs to know your concerns are serious. Avoid lecturing or arguing; state your concerns and ask him to seek help. Don't threaten to take away his control—he already feels out of control. What he needs is hope. Be ready to provide resources for him to get help, including the National Suicide Prevention Lifeline or the National Suicide and Crisis Hotline, now available nationwide by dialing 988. (See Appendix C for other resources.) Assess the immediate level of danger, and if you fear suicide may be imminent, call 911. It may very well be impossible for a mother to confront the reality that her child is in danger of taking his or her own life without being traumatized by that fact herself. That is a level of fear beyond any other. In this situation, it is not just your officer who needs to seek professional help but you also. Don't hesitate. Yes, of course you can call on your Blue Sisters; we are all there to support you, but this is a time when seeking help from someone who understands the issues you face may be best. In fact, your seeking help may encourage your officer to do the same, and you may receive advice from a counselor that will in turn help your officer. Stop at nothing to save your child.

# CHAPTER 12

# Stand Strong

One of my favorite sayings in relation to being a police mom is this:

*If he is strong enough to put on the badge, we have to be strong enough to let him.*

— Anonymous

Being the mother of an adult can be hard enough; they've become independent thinkers and make choices we may disagree with. Yet we have to let them go their own way. For a police mom that can be especially difficult. Even though our worries are significant, we no longer have the right to tell our adult sons and daughters that their path is limited by *our* fears. If law enforcement is their chosen career, *we* are the ones who have to get stronger.

## FINDING HELP FOR OUR OFFICERS

That does not mean, however, that we don't stay alert and watch them carefully for any indication of pain or suffering. We will want to be aware of and make our officers aware of resources and help available to them, should it be needed.

## Emptying the Garbage

Rarely does an officer respond to a call where all is well and everyone is safe and happy. Even routine calls—as if such a thing exists—generally drop responding officers right in the middle of someone's worst day. Even simply working a barricade well away from the scene of an incident, our officers may be subjected to anger, threats, and violence; and through it all, they must remain calm. But they often don't *feel* calm.

Professional decorum requires that they stuff all those feelings down inside and not take the bait but continue to be courteous. They often have multiple instances a day that require them to ignore their feelings, respond professionally, and just move on to the next call. So, where do all those feelings of anger, fear, guilt, disgust, or horror go?

Susan Lewis Simons, Founder and President of Under The Shield, Inc., (https://undertheshield.com) presents the best analogy in *The Simons Theory of the Psychological Garbage Can*. This theory explains what happens to those unexpressed emotions and difficult experiences by comparing one's psyche to a kitchen garbage can. All the old, dirty, messy, nasty things that we shove into our garbage can at home are not unlike all the dirty, messy, nasty things our officer encounters on the job.

He goes through his day, month, year, or career, shoving all that nastiness deep into his internal garbage can.

Think about the garbage can in your kitchen. How much nasty stuff can you cram in there? Probably quite a bit, if you keep shoving it in and pushing it deep inside. But eventually, that garbage can will hold no more, and then what happens? It begins to overflow. The mess begins to seep onto everything around it. And if you keep shoving more and more inside? Eventually, that garbage container will burst, spreading that mess all over your home. It's not too unlike Seth's garbage, as described in the previous chapter, in the form of memories, visions, emotions, and doubts, that got shoved deep down until he could no longer contain it all and he broke down. It was going to take a lot of work to repair the damage his garbage had caused—the fear he'd caused his mother, the destruction to his marriage over months of unpredictable behavior, and even the friendships he'd put in danger by withdrawing and shutting out those who cared about him.

Just like at home, however, there is a simple solution to the overflowing garbage within an officer's soul. Empty it before it gets full! Encourage your officer to develop a support system and find someone to talk to about the hard stuff. It may be a friend, coworker, relative, pastor—anyone he trusts fully and with whom he feels safe, someone who won't freak out about the stories and thoughts shared. Siblings are sometimes very good in this role. Frequently, a fellow officer or retired officer who has experienced the same things proves to be the best sounding board and support. Oftentimes an officer needs more, however. A "professional garbage collector," so to speak. But what kind of help is best in this case?

## Getting Help

Peer Counseling bridges the gap between talking to a friend and seeing a professional psychologist or therapist. In days not so long ago, and going back eons, attempts at peer support often took place in a rather casual manner, as officers gathered in parking lots or local bars to vent and talk through a tough incident. These "choir practice" sessions, as officers often referred to them to avoid the attention of their superiors, were sometimes helpful in the short term, even without trained leaders.

The biggest problem, however, was they almost always involved excessive alcohol. Too often, the result was that officers who may already have been self-medicating with alcohol went deeper down that dark hole, and the process inadvertently encouraged troubled officers to shove a traumatic event down deeper in an attempt to appear unscathed while laughing off the disturbing call. Long term, these gatherings did more harm than good. Sadly, "choir practice," by that name or any other, still takes place in many cities and towns and is not likely to be of help to your son or daughter.

In our community, our LEOs are fortunate to have a peer support organization, Mid-South First Responders Support Network, led by trained active or retired first responders. They offer regular meetings as well as personal consultations for any first responder. This group has saved many careers and marriages, not to mention the lives they have saved by listening, sharing, and supporting one another with an understanding that can only come from someone who has lived the life. A group such as this is safe, effective, and confidential, made all the more so since all members face their demons and share together. It is not operated by or associated with any police, fire, or other agency. It is true peer counseling and support. Many communities across the country have similar groups, albeit under a different name.

Not every community will have a peer support organization like this, of course. But there are national peer support groups that are available to officers in any location or community. I'm not talking about your average Facebook group or social media site, although there certainly are those and many of them are extremely helpful.

Unfortunately, there are a few of those social media groups that purport to offer online peer support but have quickly been reduced to gripe fests with shaky security and little guarantee of confidentiality. Officers should visit sites and check the level of security and confidentiality before baring their souls online. Now that I think about it, that same advice holds for in-person support groups as well. There is no need for paranoia, but caution, research, and references are appropriate in selecting whom an officer should trust.

Don't be deterred, however. There are several national peer

support groups that are excellent and above reproach in every way. They are a lifesaver to many a distraught officer. The most notable in my opinion is the aforementioned Under The Shield, Inc. Details of how to find them and other good resources can be found in Appendix C.

Other types of counseling that may be available for your officer include in-house counseling through the department in the form of mental health professionals on staff or a department chaplain. Many departments also offer an Employee Assistance Program (EAP), whereby the department pays for counseling from a contracted outside provider. And of course, there are private therapists and counselors, which some officers choose, even though it may mean out-of-pocket payments, since these counselors are not connected to the department in any way.

Is professional counseling better than peer support? It depends. For many officers, particularly the old-school veteran officer, just the suggestion of professional counseling will set off a firestorm of distrust and anger. Feelings run high, and possibly for good reason. It has only been in more recent years that law enforcement agencies have come to view counseling as an effective and wise option for a troubled officer. Previously, and possibly still in some locations or from some supervisors, it was perceived that an officer who sought professional help was weak and not up to the standards of a law enforcement agency. Officers were often disciplined or even fired for seeking the help they needed. Even worse, many officers believed that what they said to a counselor would get back to their commander and that they would be judged and punished for a conversation they had believed confidential.

Private conversations with a therapist getting back to other officers was not uncommon in the past and could be terribly destructive. However, in more recent times, following the implementation of HIPAA regulations and a greater awareness of the emotional struggles LEOs go through, this leaking of personal information has, for the most part, been eliminated. Certainly, the practice of a therapist directly reporting what is shared by any individual officer to his or her superior is reprehensible and hopefully long outdated.

Still, there are rare exceptions to a client's right to privacy. There are also differences based on the role of the therapist. An officer looking for a safe place to "empty his garbage" needs to do a little homework and even ask for referrals from a trusted source before baring his deepest feelings.

That brings us to the question of services requiring Mandatory Reporting versus those that don't. I'm not saying that one is better than the other, just that you and your officer should understand the difference and know what you're getting into when you choose a counselor, therapist, coach, or support group. Any *licensed* psychologist, psychiatrist, social worker, therapist, or counselor is a Mandatory Reporter. That means if they are told or have knowledge of an individual being in danger of causing harm to himself or others, they are required by law to report it to law enforcement and certain others. These professionals may work in a hospital or clinic setting or have a private practice and, depending on what letters follow their name, they may be able to prescribe medications or affiliate with someone who can.

An *unlicensed* counselor, on the other hand, is not required to make such a report. Nor are they allowed to prescribe medications or perform certain treatments. That does not mean, however, that they are not qualified to offer counseling, coaching, guidance, and support. In fact, they may be more qualified. These are often the people who have lived the life, understand the pain and the challenges, and can offer genuine support. These are the peer support groups, stress coaches, and self-help groups like Under the Shield Foundation and Alcoholics Anonymous. What is best for any individual depends on the specific person and situation. The bottom line is that there is help available for your officer and for you. If you believe your officer needs help but refuses to talk to anyone, get help for yourself!

## WHO IS THERE FOR YOU?

When this police life becomes too much, there are a number of groups, organizations, and agencies that are there to assist you through these hard times. They may, in fact, find you before you even have time to search for help.

Of course, we've already talked about police mom groups and friends, and we are indeed here for you when bad things happen. Some of us have been through the worst and can offer understanding and advice based on experience. But in all honesty, practical help may be better found from other sources.

## Your Officer's Department

Whatever the crisis you are facing, remember that in most cases one of your greatest allies and supporters will be the department or agency your officer works for. (Yes, there are times when it is the department that is the problem or a part of the problem, but that is not the norm.) From your officer's co-workers and lieutenants up through the chain of command to the very top, you will find officers standing with you, helping to navigate the hard times. Don't make the mistake of turning them away. They are likely also concerned for your officer and want him safe, healthy, and back on the job. They will be there to guide and support you and your officer's family through the trying times of an officer's physical and emotional recovery.

## The Union

Most larger cities have their own police union, while others use the services of a state or national law enforcement union such as the Fraternal Order of Police (FOP). Smaller agencies may not be unionized at all, so you will want to learn early on in your officer's career what, if any, union he or she belongs to. Know how to contact them quickly should the need arise.

The services they offer will vary, but it's good to know what kind of things they can help with. Some services are standard among all, but union contracts with each municipality or agency will spell out the details. Ask your officer or go on the union website to learn more.

Among the most common union services is representation of an officer in the event of an officer-involved shooting or accusation of use of unnecessary force. In these cases, your officer's union representative will show up on scene or contact him or her directly as quickly as possible. They will advise your officer of his rights and stand with your officer during any questioning, helping to provide legal representation if needed. Because what they hear from your officer or others is confidential, they will not be able to tell you much about the details of an incident, but they will talk to you about what is happening and what to expect as far as procedures. Rest assured, the union is on the side of your officer.

The union is also there for the officer and the family in the case of a serious injury or death. A union representative may show up at the hospital and stay with you as much as you need them. They will shield you from the media and unwanted visitors, bring you coffee, and hold your hand. They will inform you about insurance and help you navigate that system and may even conduct fundraising activities to help with expenses. Should your officer die in the line of duty, your union rep will possibly be the person by your side, helping to plan the funeral and arrange for guests' accommodations, speakers, transportation, and anything else you need. And they will not abandon you the day after the funeral. They will help to coordinate death benefits from the department, city, and other institutions and will continue to be one of your most dependable connections to the department throughout the following years.

## C.O.P.S.

Concerns of Police Survivors or C.O.P.S. (http://www.concernsofpolicesurvivors.org) provides resources to help the families (spouses, children, parents, siblings, and significant others) of officers who have died in the line of duty to rebuild their shattered lives. C.O.P.S. is a national organization with more than 50 chapters across the country that work with local survivors. This organization has been a godsend for family members as they find comfort among others who have suffered a line-of-duty loss.

C.O.P.S. programs include the National Police Survivors' Conference held each May during National Police Week; scholarships; peer support at the national, state, and local levels; "C.O.P.S. Kids" counseling reimbursement program; "C.O.P.S. Kids" Summer Camp; "C.O.P.S. Teens" Outward Bound Adventure for young adults; special retreats for spouses, parents, siblings, adult children, extended family, and co-workers; and other assistance programs, all at no cost. C.O.P.S. helps families and co-workers learn to navigate their grief, honor their fallen hero, and connect with other survivors who have walked a similar path. Peer support is the heart of this organization.

## THE STRENGTH WITHIN YOU

Have you ever caught yourself saying, "Oh, I would never have the strength she does," when observing someone go through a really difficult situation? I have a surprise for you. That person didn't think she could be that strong either. But when life gives us no acceptable alternative, the huge majority of us will find within ourselves the strength to handle what we must.

I learned this the hard way through a life that has given me a few significant bumps and bruises. Whether it was losing a job, finding myself divorced and alone with a new baby and a toddler, or losing my youngest son to cancer at just four years old, I never saw any option other than to handle it. Perhaps other people saw that as being strong, but I saw it as doing what I had to. I'm sure you've had your own life challenges. You have found strength before and you will again.

When your officer is in crisis, you will take a deep breath, pull that strength from deep inside, and take care of business. You will. Never doubt yourself. Doubt can waste precious time. Just know you have the strength within you.

This is a good time to remind yourself that you are not alone. Whatever the crisis, help and support are available. Lean on those who care about you; pull strength from their love. Listen to information and advice from the experts and know that your instincts will guide you. Whatever this police life throws at you, you've got this.

# CHAPTER 13

# A Word for Dads

So much of what I've written throughout this book is applicable for dads also. All the information about what your officer is going through, how she will change, what to expect—all your questions will likely be answered throughout the book, so feel free to go back and read from the beginning. Much of what you read here will also help you understand your wife's perspective. But this chapter, I hope, will go a step further in addressing the unique role of a cop's dad.

Here's the thing. I'm not a dad. I cannot fully understand or experience the same things you do. To write this chapter, I have relied heavily on words from others in your position—dads of police officers all across the country. I've also spoken to police officers whose dads have been a critical component in their support network and to those who have not been fortunate enough to have a father to support them. I can conclude from all I've heard that as much as a mother's love and support means, a dad's pride, confidence, and backing is a gift every officer values. Let me say this more clearly—you matter!

## NOT JUST MOMS IN BOXER SHORTS

Your feelings and reactions to your officer's life will be different than your wife's. The most obvious being you are not as likely to show your emotions or voice your worries. Pacing the floor or working with your hands is more of a dad's style of worrying—something to keep busy and distract you from the thoughts running through your head. But let's be honest, sometimes that nagging concern in the back of your mind can turn into full-blown fear for the well-being of your son or daughter. A dad is a parent too, and most dads feel a heavy burden of responsibility to keep the family safe. That's quite a load to carry, especially when your offspring steps into the very admirable but dangerous role of law enforcement.

As one MPD dad explained to me, "I'm not all touchy-feely. I don't think about how I feel, I just do what I do." That dad probably expressed the feelings (Oops, not *feelings*—I should have said *point of view*!) of most dads, police family or not. What impressed me, however, was when he went on to say, "I raised my daughter to follow her own path and make her own decisions. I trust her to do that. I'll support her whatever her journey. She chose a tough career. I don't worry about her because I know she is well trained and capable. But if she ever needs me, I'll be there for her." Oh, if only we could all think like this dad.

## A Dad's Concerns

I think men, in general, are more pragmatic in their thinking than many women, resulting in police dads taking a more practical and less emotional view of police life. This is not always true, of course, but often a dad will look at the facts, find the information he needs, and accept what he believes to be true—police officers are well trained, are probably in the best physical condition of their lives, have backup from other officers, most likely have built strong community relationships, and are ready and able to do this job. And with those facts, a dad concludes there is little cause for worry.

In all my interviews, dads consistently expressed they had been more concerned about their sons and daughters *before* they went into law enforcement. They worried, or at least wondered, would this young person find her calling, would she be happy in her career, and would she be rewarded for her talents? It seems that going into law enforcement was the answer in many dads' eyes. Now they could relax and be proud of the person they raised.

Still, there is a lot to be concerned about with a son or daughter in law enforcement. One of those very pragmatic dads I spoke with explained, "I could worry about every call he goes on or each encounter he has with a bad guy, but it would just be wasted energy. He could just as likely get hurt driving to work or going hunting on his day off. We have to respect the professionals they are and let them do their jobs. I'd rather think about how much he enjoys his work and how good he is at it."

This same dad went on to say, "Yeah, when I hear about an officer being injured or some mass shooting taking place, I do get concerned. And I wait for that text from my kid letting me know he's okay."

It seems all parents rely on that quick communication, usually in the form of a text message, from their officer in times of crisis. Don't hesitate to let your officer know how important that message is to you and your family.

Russell is the father of two officers working two different jobs, one with a large city department and the other with the county in which that city lies. The "boys," as he tends to refer to his officers, share an apartment and often unload on each other, discussing the calls, the criminals, the bureaucracy of their respective agencies, and the occasional case they work together. Russell explained that his biggest worry is the two "boys" working a scene together and possibly witnessing their brother getting shot.

He says, "It's the psychological injuries I worry about. My boys are tough, and they are both good cops. But I don't know how either of them could go on if something happened to the other. It's the things they see and what gets in their heads. I see the changes in both of them over time, and that worries me. I just hope they come out the other end of this career the same people they went in as."

When I asked Russell if he worried about his sons getting injured, he responded, "Nah, they can take care of themselves.

I know it can happen, but it's not something I think about."

Russell's concerns about the psychological damage officers endure are common among LEO dads. Perhaps that's because a dad can teach a kid to fight, to protect himself physically. He can see that his officer is trained well, can handle his weapon, and is in good physical condition, so he can trust those things. But there is no way a parent can imagine or prepare a son or daughter for the terrible sights they see and trauma they encounter on the job. For a father, programmed to protect them, it is often those experiences beyond his control that concern him the most.

## Working Through the Worries

For many men, understanding a situation is all that is needed to resolve their concerns. Their sense of calm comes from knowledge. Several of the dads I spoke to said they watch the local news so they can stay abreast of what's happening in their officer's jurisdiction. Some even enjoy listening to the police scanner—that evil device that I tell all parents to avoid. But if that is what brings you comfort, go for it.

Other dads work through their worries, or distract themselves from them, with a variety of projects, hobbies, and activities. Physical activity seems to be the key. It's easy enough to bury yourself in your work or an absorbing hobby but be sure to stay connected to your family along the way. Keep in mind that if you are worried, your wife, grandkids, and officer's spouse are likely equally or even more concerned. If you can involve your family in activities that keep you all calm, everyone wins.

Police dads are forced to realize that there are things they can control and things they cannot. As one dad put it, the Serenity Prayer taught in Alcoholics Anonymous meetings around the world carries a valuable message: *God, grant me the serenity to accept the things I cannot change, courage to change the things I can, and wisdom to know the difference.* So, whether your inspiration comes from a prayer or life experience, it's wise to know that this career is the choice of the man or woman you raised. They knew and accepted the risks it carries and the challenges it presents. It is theirs. You can let this particular worry go, knowing your officer has it covered.

## SUPPORTING YOUR OFFICER

Moms make cookies and tell their officers they are proud of them. Dads give a nod. Okay, that may be an oversimplification of the difference in how moms and dads show their support for their officers, but it's not far from the truth. A dad's support tends to be quieter, although certainly no less genuine or strong. Mom may bring home books to read and decals for the cars, she may order the t-shirt for Dad that matches her own, and maybe Dad will go along and wear the shirt and display the decals with pride. Maybe he'll even read the books. But Dad's support for his officer son or daughter is likely to be more private, just between them. The officer will feel it, for certain, but the rest of the world may not see it.

One of our local dads explained to me, "We talk. My job is to listen when she wants to talk about things that happen, and I just let her talk it out. We talk about career choices that come up, and I support her decisions. She knows I'm always here for her."

There are, however, many things a dad can do to show his support for his officer in other ways. Dads too may enjoy doing a ride-along to experience their officer's day. Dads may enjoy participating in a Citizen's Police Academy course at your local department. These hands-on experiences in understanding the world in which our officers work will demonstrate your interest and support and are always fun. Dads can also serve as volunteers at a precinct or police station, doing tasks such as minor repairs, clean up, and even helping with precinct cookouts or other special events. Just head down to the precinct and offer to pitch in.

That concept of just being there for your officer is huge. There is no better way to support your officer. Maybe you are the person your officer can confide in when he needs to talk out a tough day. Just listen. You can reinforce that the decisions he made and actions he took were good solid choices. If your officer is ever truly troubled by an incident, encourage him to seek help through peer support groups or professional counseling. Surround your officer with love and encouragement. And always remember that a father's pride is the most treasured gift you will ever give to your officer or any son or daughter.

Don't hesitate to say the words, "I am proud of the person you are and the job you do."

## SUPPORTING YOUR WIFE

I can only imagine how hard it is for a dad to comfort a police officer's mother who is chronically frightened by her son's or daughter's job. I know a few dads who have been in that position. It must be hard to not be able to relieve her fears when you feel that responsibility to protect your family. I can tell you that the best thing you can do is to encourage her to find and join a police moms group. This may be one of those situations when her comfort needs to come from someone other than you. It is, however, your encouragement that may get her there. I have listed resources for her and you in Appendix C.

Then there are those occasions when an incident in your community—a police-involved shooting or an officer down—has you both worried about your officer's possible involvement and safety. Until you get that all-important text or call from your officer saying he is okay, all you can do is wait. Remember that your officer is likely very busy when a major incident occurs, not necessarily because he was involved in the incident but because he is working the after-incident scene or covering a larger patrol area so others can work the scene. He may be at the hospital with an injured officer or with family members of that officer. He may be directing traffic around the location or writing witness reports. His failure to contact you immediately does not mean he was injured. In most cases, it simply means he is busy.

Remind your wife of the many things that could be keeping your officer occupied. I always tell parents not to call their officers repeatedly should they hear of an incident. That said, if you have not heard from your officer in about thirty minutes, a text message asking him to confirm his safety is a less intrusive way of reaching out and is a reasonable request of your officer. Of course, if you haven't heard anything within that thirty minutes, you could also be fairly confident by then that the involved officer's family has been notified, meaning your officer most likely is safe.

Donald is a dad in our local parents' group. He shared that over the many years of his marriage he has learned that the best way to comfort and support his wife when she is upset about anything is to just listen. Let her express her concerns but know that you don't have to fix every problem. It may be that your wife just needs to vent. Give her that. Her worries about your officer's job or the events that occur on that job are not problems to be solved. They may just be feelings and thoughts that your wife needs to express. Listen. Commiserate. Agree. Then wrap your arms around her and tell her it will be okay.

Dads, I hope you don't just read this chapter because your wife handed it to you and said you should. Although I've tried to target these last few pages to address a dad's unique position in a police family, the other information and advice throughout this book will largely apply to you too. If you haven't already, go back and start at the beginning.

# CHAPTER 14

# For Police Wives

We often talk about our officers as heroes, but I've learned that behind many heroes you will find the source of their super-power—their spouse. Police wives hold more power and more responsibility than the world knows. So let me pay homage to our police wives. You are the strongest women I know.

You may not always feel that strength inside you, of course, and you may face many of the same questions and concerns as your mother-in-law. I encourage you to read other sections of this book—in particular, the Chapter 5 sections on Husbands, Wives, and Children—or better yet, go back and read the entire book. You may find a lot of answers throughout these pages.

## THE SECOND HARDEST JOB ON EARTH

Not every woman is cut out to be married to a law enforcement officer; not every woman has what it takes. Oh, there are the *badge bunnies*, the women who are attracted to the uniform more than the person wearing it and believe life with an LEO will be filled with prestige and excitement. That woman will be gone within two years. To be a real police wife takes strength, in every sense of the word. It requires independence and confidence, although those characteristics can be built over time. It also takes compassion, understanding, flexibility, creativity, and lots of patience. Perhaps most of all, it requires a sense of humor. It's going to be a wild ride.

You may doubt you have all those characteristics, and you may worry about how to make it work with rotating shifts, daycare for your little ones, and your own job that your family depends on to help cover the bills. Going into life as a police family, you don't need to have all the answers or be as strong as the experienced police wives appear to be. You do, however, need to have the capacity to develop those things. You'll have help along the way—from your officer, your department, your family, and those experienced police wives you see. Time on the job will offer plenty of opportunities to learn, but the truth is, you are taking on the second hardest job on earth. (The first, of course, is that of your officer.)

## Loving and Living with a Police Officer

If you are newly married to an officer, or if your husband has recently joined law enforcement, you may be surprised by the culture, the changes that develop in your officer, and the impact this job will have on your family life. I encourage you to refer to Chapter 4 regarding the changes your officer will likely go through and the causes and benefits of them. One thing I can assure you is that this job—this life—is different. It will change you right along with your officer, and together you will become a police family. But so too will your children, in-laws, and extended family. Together, you will all join with other families in your department and across the nation to become part of the Thin Blue Line.

As you see the changes in your new officer, remind yourself that he now works in an environment that demands he be on high alert throughout his shift. It can take a while before he adjusts to the more relaxed environment of home. Give him time. Allow him an extra thirty minutes or an hour to switch gears when he arrives home. Avoid peppering him with questions or telling him about your day the minute he walks in the door. That investment in time will reap great rewards in your relationship.

If you live with the constant worry and fear that many loved ones experience, you will need to find ways to take control of your fears in a way that does not distract your officer from his responsibilities on the job. You may benefit from the advice for moms on managing your fears and adjusting to police life in Chapters 6 through 9. And you will need to work with your husband to identify the things you can each do to ease your worries.

## Making It Work for You and Your Officer

Communication is the key to a happy marriage. How many times have you heard that and wondered, "How am I supposed to communicate with a man I rarely see?" There are many forms of communication, of course, and good communication takes more than talking. There are far more nonverbal than verbal messages shared in a marriage. Think about what you are saying with your actions, expressions, and attitude. Are you saying what you mean to?

*"Oops, I didn't mean to make that expression out loud!"*

— Anonymous

For our purposes here, we are talking about verbal conversation. I talked about communication in Chapter 7, but let's look at this specifically from the wife's point of view. As you adjust to the changes in your officer and try to figure out how to meet the needs of everyone in your family, you'll need to determine what those needs may be. What will work for you, your officer, and your children?

Be honest with yourself. Do you want your officer to talk to you about the things he saw and did on a rough day? Do you really want to hear the details of a horrible car crash where victims die on scene? Do you want to know that a criminal fired a gun at your officer? Or that he got his cruiser up to 125 mph during a chase? Not every police wife can hear these stories without it increasing her anxiety. Only you can determine your comfort level for work-related details, and it's up to you to be honest with your officer. If you are comfortable with, say, stories about car crashes and suspects being apprehended, but not the times your officer's life is in jeopardy, tell him so. Just remember, what your officer chooses to talk about or share with you is ultimately up to him.

There will be calls that your officer cannot talk about. He may need time to process and recover from a stress-filled event. Give him time to decompress, even if you are anxious to hear details. Let him talk only when and if he is ready which, for some events, may be never. It may be that when he does talk about certain things, he will choose someone other than you. Maybe a friend, fellow officers, or even a trusted professional. It's important that your officer has an outlet for the things that weigh on his mind. There is a section in Chapter 12 on getting help when needed.

Encourage your officer to maintain his personal friendships, both with officers who understand what he is going through and with his non-cop friends. In fact, it may be those old high school or college friends who are best able to help him blow off steam in a positive way and stay grounded to the person with whom you first fell in love. Too often, wives feel left out when their spouse spends time with friends, but for officers, it may be the very thing that preserves your marriage. Those hobbies, games, and days on the lake can be very beneficial for an officer who works under such stressful conditions. Embrace the time your officer spends with friends and the time he takes for himself. You will likely find a better partner in the man who has taken the time to care for himself.

Of course, on the other side of that issue lies *single parent syndrome.* You are not single; you are happily married, but none of your friends have ever met your husband because he is never around. The PTA parents wonder why little Tommy's dad never volunteers at school, and the teacher is not completely convinced that Tommy's dad is even real.

Yes, it can at times feel like you are a single parent, and that's not fair. You may not even be able to remember your last date night. It is important to keep your officer engaged at home and protect your time together, even while sharing him with the world. This is the realization that it was not just your husband who became a police officer. This is a role for each of you, as you all serve in a police family.

The adjustments to your lives don't have to be difficult, however. Whereas Daddy may not be able to make it to Little League practice or PTA meetings, he might be able to do the morning drop-off at school so he can meet the teachers and feel a part of his child's life. Date nights don't always have to be at night. A weekday brunch before shift or quick meet up for lunch in a parking lot during shift offer the same private time to reconnect with your hero husband. Once again, creativity can save the day. Some of these outside-the-box solutions may become treasured family traditions over the years and even strengthen family bonds.

I need to mention your officer's partners and the relationship they share. Those are some of the closest bonds he will have. It may be hard for you to understand that brotherhood until you see it in action, but when your officer calls for backup in the midst of a life or death struggle, it is his fellow officers who will be there for him, just as he will be there for them in any crisis.

You may have strong feelings about a female officer being partnered with your husband. You may struggle with jealousy over the time they spend together and the relationship they build. You may also worry whether she will be able to help your officer when help is needed. I can assure you that your husband's female partner is far more qualified than you may think, and she can and will put her life on the line to protect him if necessary.

No woman goes through the rigorous training and hard work (much of it creating a less than flattering look) to become a police officer, just to find a man. A female officer is there to do the same job as your husband, is equally qualified, and has no interest in undermining her job or her relationship with her partner by becoming involved with a married man. Just like her male counterparts, she considers her partner (your husband) a brother.

All that has been written in this book, although aimed specifically at your officer's mother, is good information for you too, and I encourage you to read earlier chapters that may apply. There are also several books written for police wives that I recommend. Many of these bring in the two components that may be key to making police life work for you: humor and faith. They are included in Appendix C.

Police humor is a strange thing. You may find yourself laughing at things that in earlier times you never would have thought funny. When your garbage disposal breaks and the plumber finds an unspent bullet is the culprit, all you can do is laugh. When your three-year-old asks loudly in the dollar store checkout line, "Can I get handcuffs, Mom? I won't mix them up with Daddy's," you can only shrug and smile at the staring strangers. And the retelling of the story about your undercover husband picking up a hooker will never be funnier than when told at the PTA meeting. It is the ability to laugh at the absurd, somewhat twisted life we live that keeps us sane.

When laughing doesn't work, we turn to faith. Have faith in your God to watch over your officer and bring him home safe. Have faith in his training, that he knows what to do and how to do it in the moment it is needed. Have faith that his FTO has taught your officer to apply his training in the real world and have faith in his fellow officers that they will always have his back. And have faith in yourself that you are the right person to be a police wife; you have, or will learn, what it takes to do this job.

## YOUR CHILDREN

Your officer's job will impact every member of your family. Your children will have to adjust to all the changes that come in routines, schedules, and family traditions. They will face their own emotions and worries about their officer parent. If you stay attuned to their feelings and listen to their needs, you will be able to reassure them and resolve any issues.

It's important that the information children hear about

high-profile events, locally or nationally, comes from the adults who love them, not the TV news or the kids at school. I have a friend who had a startling awakening in this regard. Her almost three-year-old was absorbed in playing with her dolls on the floor in the room where my friend was watching the news. The little girl turned to her mommy and asked, "Is Daddy going to die too?" My friend was stunned. She had no idea her two-year-old daughter was listening to the TV or was even capable of understanding the report about two police officers in another city who were shot and killed.

Many kids have misconceptions about the job of a police officer, believing their days are filled with violence and danger. That can bring undue worry. The truth is that most officers' days are much more mundane than a child's imagination would have them believe, so talk to your kids about what a normal day might be. Let them visit the precinct to see dad at work. If your child is worried about Dad's safety, assure her that Daddy is very well trained and good at his job. Remind her there are many other officers who work with her daddy and will be there whenever he needs backup. Avoid promises that may be impossible to keep, so instead of saying that Dad will not get hurt, let your children know that Daddy loves them very much and will always do everything within his power to come home safely to them.

A child who can't sleep at night because Daddy is not home may need a promise that he will come kiss her goodnight when he gets home, even if it is long after bedtime and she is already asleep. Should she wake up, I assure you she will go right back to sleep feeling more secure and content. A child who wants Dad to read him a bedtime story may settle for a recorded version of that story. One police dad read the entire Harry Potter series to his two children via video, one chapter at a time over a period of two years, recording each night's reading in advance and sending the video to his sons' tablet each evening, along with a goodnight message.

As hard as it is for a parent working the three-to-eleven shift to miss their child's T-ball and soccer games, dance recitals, and first dates, it is even harder on the child who doesn't understand why their friend's dad can take off work early to be there but his cannot. That child still yearns for Dad's attention and pride, so don't leave Dad out. Record those events so your officer can at least watch later and share his pride with his children. You can even make a short recording of Dad wishing his son luck or giving a valuable tip to be shared before the big game or beaming with pride and telling his daughter she is beautiful before prom.

All those messages are even better in a video call where Dad can be "present," albeit by phone. But because Dad may have to respond to a call at the exact moment his daughter descends the stairs in her prom dress, a prerecorded message is the next best thing—along with a little personal time after the fact to hear all about it.

## YOUR MOTHER-IN-LAW

In most families, your mother-in-law can be your closest ally and greatest source of comfort and help as you navigate this world of law enforcement. She is, after all, the most like you in her love and concern for your officer's well-being. She loves your children as only a grandmother can, and she loves you. Allow her in, share your concerns, and let her be your rock. Then turn the tables, and you be there for her. She will need you. Together, the two of you can support one another, your officer, and your family. But sadly, not all families share a bond that will allow that.

When I first started working with police families, I was shocked and saddened to hear young wives talk about the strained relationships they had with their officer's mother. Of course, I know not all mothers- and daughters-in-law get along, but it seemed there was an abundance of in-law problems in the law enforcement world. Then I started noticing what was really going on. It's too often a competitive world with our officers caught in the middle.

On the surface, it's simply about time. Your officer, who used to have plenty of free time in the evenings and weekends to hang out with his family, now finds himself working those evening hours, stretching his energy over double shifts, working through holidays, weekends, dance recitals, family traditions, and birthday parties. Then he comes home exhausted and feeling guilty, knowing he has to be back on duty in just a few hours. His children need time with their dad. His wife is lonely and frustrated. His mom complains she hasn't seen him in weeks and is hurt by his absence. Even his friends get in on the deal and make him feel bad for not making it to their regular poker game.

In an effort to appease everyone, our officer hero, who is definitely not feeling like a hero to anyone at this point, carves out little bits of time for everyone but satisfies no one. He finally gives up trying to please everyone and goes to bed. Our police mom blames the wife for taking up his time and causing him to cancel their lunch plans. Our police wife believes she and the children should come first, so she leaves Mom out of their usual Sunday dinner. And the group of friends? They are left out altogether. Now everyone is disappointed, hurt, and angry. Sound familiar?

Too often the competition goes much deeper than time with your officer. Between mothers of sons and the women their sons marry, it can become a competition of love. Wives can become defensive; mothers can become overly protective. Both suffer from jealousy. If a man chooses to spend time with his mother, he may be accused of being a *momma's boy* and his mom is accused of not letting go. If he gives up some of the time he had previously spent with his mom to now build a life with his wife, she may be accused of manipulating him to get her way. All I can say to this chain of events is *stop it!* I cannot imagine how painful it would be to co-exist in a family where all are not valued and appreciated and where a mother's love is pitted against a life partner's. No officer deserves to be put in that situation.

Here's what a wife should know about the mother of her

police officer husband. That mom loves your husband in the exact same way you love your own child. No difference. Just as you miss your little one when he is out of your sight, so does your officer's mom. Just as you would do anything to protect your baby, so would your mother-in-law. Those feelings of love, adoration, and protection do not disappear with age.

As mothers, we hopefully learn to behave appropriately and recognize that you, his wife, now come first in his life. We allow our adult children to lead independent lives, but our feelings simply do not go away. When our children grow up and take on dangerous roles, we feel an overpowering need to make sure they are safe, physically and psychologically. We worry when they face a specific danger or when it's just been so long since we've seen them that we have no way of knowing if they are all right. The more we are left out of our officers' lives, the more we worry. Worry becomes fear, and fear is too often expressed as anger.

The obvious solution happens to also be the easiest. If there is tension between the mother and wife in a man's life, the easiest solution for both is to simply accept that this other woman loves the same man you love but poses no threat to your relationship. None. There is room for both women—mother and wife—in a man's life and in his heart.

By accepting the mother who raised your officer, even welcoming her into your own heart and home, you are giving a beautiful gift, not just to her but to your husband. It is a fortunate man who can be surrounded by women who love him and care about his well-being. And it is the fortunate mom who can expand her love for her son to include the woman he has chosen in life.

So please, be kind and generous to your mother-in-law with your time, with your officer's time, and with the love and acceptance of your family. I promise you, if you love her son and bring happiness to his life, your mother-in-law will, in all likelihood, come to love you as well.

# CHAPTER 15

# Attention, Officers!

If you are a law enforcement officer reading this, it is probably because your mother handed it to you. I can already see your eyes rolling as you think there is nothing I, the mother of another officer, could say that will be useful to you. And you may be right. But the Memphis Police Department thought it was worthwhile to have me teach a class for the recruits in their academy, so let's appease your mom and give it a shot.

If you have completed your academy training in the last few years, you were likely told something regarding the impact this job can have on your family. You've been told that becoming a police officer will affect you personally—it will change you. As you change, so too will your family as they adapt to your schedule, your needs, and your moods. They will become a Police Family, and that may be a concept you have not thought about.

This book is divided into chapters and sections all outlined in the Table of Contents. I encourage you to look through it and find the topics that might be of interest to you. We've been talking about you a great deal, and you might want to know what's been said. You may even come to understand your mom's perspective—her worries and fears—and learn what advice has been given to her within these pages. I hope you find it interesting. But there are a few topics that I believe are important enough to pull out and repeat here, *just for you*. Listen up!

## A PARENT'S PRIDE

I'm willing to bet that your mom and dad have told you they are proud of you. But I want you to really hear that. They have been proud of you since you were born, but the day you pinned on that badge and began this job to protect and serve, their pride soared to new levels in the stratosphere. I want you to remember that. When your mom is worried—and worry, she will—and asks questions you don't want to answer or tells you she is afraid you will get injured, know that the one thing greater than her worry and fear is her pride. It's a pride like none you've ever felt from your parents before. Accept it. You've earned it. It's a feeling they deserve to have, and one you deserve as well.

## CHANGES IN YOU AND THOSE WHO LOVE YOU

I'm sure you've already noticed them—the little changes in your behavior that mark you as a cop. You always sit facing the door in a restaurant. You wolf down your food like you're in some kind of competition to finish first. You quickly size up people you meet, even off duty, and know right away if the kid dating your teenage daughter can be trusted. Most of these small changes will have little impact on your family, but other transformations occur that may mean big changes for those you love.

The people who care about you will try to interpret your new behaviors and adapt to what you need. They want to make your life easier. The problem is, they cannot read your mind and probably don't know what you need. They will on occasion guess wrong and do the one thing you wish they wouldn't. Try to remember, you're not the only one learning a new role as you step into the job of law enforcement. Your family is also learning—learning how to become a Police Family.

Your family will, over time, adjust to your long hours and crazy schedule. They will learn the language and figure out solutions to the new challenges they face. But you need to give them time, just as your department is providing you time to learn. The difference is, they do not receive formal training for their new roles.

As family members adapt to this new life, you will likely see changes in them also. Perhaps your husband has learned to make a perfect French braid in your nine-year-old's hair or she now prefers his version of a bed-time story because he makes the voices better. Your wife may learn to fix the toilet and help with 6th grade homework, because those things need to be done even when you are not there. These changes can lead to a new-found independence in those you always felt were dependent upon you. They may also lead to some resentment over the extra workload or your possible lack of awareness regarding the additional weight your spouse now carries. I encourage you to pay attention to what your spouse is doing.

Remember too, your wife (or husband) will have their own

emotions to deal with, including a strange mixture of pride, fear, confusion, loneliness, resentment, jealousy, and excitement. As you settle into your job, worry and fear will possibly prevail. These feelings are real, constant, and justified for every person who loves a police officer. Please don't discount or trivialize them. And when fear or other confusing emotions kick in, that is the time patience, acceptance, and communication are most important.

Your children will feel the changes in you and other family members as well, although their reactions will depend a great deal on their ages. From infancy through adolescence, your children will react to the new routines, schedules, and moods. Refer to the sections in Chapter 4 regarding the impact of the job on the rest of your family. Your understanding of the ways in which your family is affected is critical to meeting their needs.

You may or may not have a spouse and children but, if you are reading this book, it is most likely that you have a mother. Maybe a father as well. They too are affected by your career. Aside from the great pride they felt when you became an officer, I can assure you that they also worry. Your parents are going to be afraid for your safety most of all. They are going to be concerned about the changes they see in you—the stress you feel, the tiredness they see in your eyes, the things you have seen and experienced that will change you forever.

Know this: You cannot protect your family from being affected by your job. I've heard many an officer, usually those old dogs who have been on the department since the middle ages, say they will *"leave their families out of it."* Can't be done! This is your life now and trying to do so would leave your family out of your life.

It's not just you who became an officer. Your family has become a Police Family. Most of the time that's a positive thing. It's a source of pride; a very special role. It can be a hard role, but it can also be rewarding for everyone in your family. Embrace your Police Family. They deserve your pride.

## YOU AND YOUR FAMILY

First, remember *you* are now part of a Police Family. You are not alone in figuring out what works for your family, and you do not have to have all the answers. Work together. Talk with your family. Tell them what you need, ask what they need, and be specific. Remember, no one can read your mind, and you can't read theirs. I can offer a few tips, however, that may help.

As you talk to your family members about what they need for this life to work, find out what is important to each person, and try to respect those needs. Does your wife need to hear "I love you" before you leave for work each day, even if it means calling her office? Does your spouse want to meet your work partner so they know who will have your back on the job? Do your kids need a goodnight kiss, even though you don't get home until long after bedtime? Do you need thirty minutes alone when you get home to shake off the day and make the switch from officer to husband and father? Does your mom need a quick text when you get off work so that she knows you are safe and headed home? All of those things are easy to fulfill, but only if you know what each person needs. Chapter 9 goes into great detail about defining and meeting the needs of your family, and Chapter 14 does so specifically for police wives.

## YOUR MOM

This book is, after all, for and about your mom, so she deserves a bit of attention here. And perhaps I can provide a little insight as to what has been going on with her since you pinned on the badge.

No matter how hardcore and tough you are, you will always be your mother's child. It doesn't matter how old you are or what you do with your life. Moms are hardwired to always want to protect and provide for their children. Therefore, your mom *will* be worried about you. No matter what you say or don't say, and regardless of how hard she works to hide it, she will be concerned every time you leave for work. If you're lucky, she won't show it too overtly. But she may. I've heard some pretty crazy stories from moms themselves relating to how they handle their fears.

She may lie awake all night waiting for you to come home. She may text you repeatedly during your shift, just to check on how you are doing. She may call multiple times, with little regard to your responsibilities on the job. She may drive around your precinct looking for your car, just to see that you are okay.

(No, I'm not kidding. It happens!) And I assure you, I've told her these reactions to her fear are not appropriate. Of course the majority of moms don't go to those extremes, and the whole purpose of this book is to help moms adapt to police life and manage their worries.

Throughout the pages of this book, I have told your mom that it is *her* responsibility to control her fear. She cannot put that responsibility on you. Your job is to, well, do your job. Her job is to let you. However, there is *one* occasion when a mother's fear may be beyond her control, and it *does* fall on you to put her at ease.

As soon as she hears about an officer down, your mom is going to become frightened. It won't matter if the incident occurred in another part of town from your location. It won't matter if the reporter stated it was a male officer and you are female. It might not even matter if she knows you are off that day. When that kind of fear grips a mother's heart, she knows only that she needs to hear your voice.

She will start by picking up the phone and trying to call you. When she can't reach you, she may continue calling, then texting, and then calling again. She could even call your precinct, your partner, your lieutenant, or your colonel. You see where this is going. But *you* can stop her. In this case, it is you, and only you, who can control her fear and her phone calls.

At the first sign of a news camera at the scene or a statement by the department about an officer being injured, you can make her life and yours easier. This is the one and only time the responsibility to control her worry is on you, and it's easy. *Call your mom!*

Just make a quick call to say, "I'm okay," or send a text with a thumbs-up emoji. Any communication from you that tells her you are all right is all that is needed. Because absolutely all she needs is to know that you are safe.

## TAKING CARE OF YOU

You cannot do your job and take care of your family unless you first take care of yourself, not just physically, but mentally too. Take time to relax. Have regular activities that you do alone and those you do as a family—things that have nothing to do with police work. A hobby allows you to focus on something else and get the stresses of the day out of your system. And time spent being truly present with your family is more valuable than anything else you can do for yourself and them.

Hold onto your friendships with your non-cop friends. A day of fishing with a buddy or a regular poker game with old friends may be the thing that best keeps you grounded and reminds you who you are underneath the badge. Letting go of the stress, staying in shape, eating well, connecting with family, having fun—those are the things that will enable you to be a great cop and, at the same time, a great son or daughter, spouse, parent, and friend. However, it's that "letting go of stress" part that can be a real challenge for a cop.

One of the things your mom and everyone else—including

you—will have legitimate concerns about is your psychological well-being. Even your department knows the risk is high enough to warrant discussing the issue in the academy and at in-service training. They likely provide options for you to get help when the pressures of the job build up. So it certainly deserves a moment of our time here.

You already know the many things that bring on stress—the long hours, lack of sleep, financial concerns, family troubles, and most certainly the things that you encounter on the job. You have hopefully found ways to cope and manage these stressors on your own through activities you enjoy and having someone you can talk with when you just need to unload. Those everyday coping mechanisms work well up to a point, but what happens when you need more?

Your department likely provides access to counseling through an EAP or similar program. There are pros and cons to utilizing these services, just as there are in seeking any form of counseling. And before you say, "I would never go to a counselor," let me point out that not all *counseling* involves a *professional counselor*. I highly recommend you go back to Chapter 11 in this book and read the section on *The Things We Don't Know to Fear*. It is written for moms, but the information there pertains to you.

So, while you are still trying to imagine any scenario in which you may need to seek help coping with your job, let me explain why, at some point in their career, virtually every officer needs *someone* to talk with, be it a coworker, friend, peer support group, or professional.

You know the calls; the DV call where the victim turns on you for arresting her abuser; the "peaceful protest" where you were spit on, cursed at, and blamed for all that's wrong in the world; the car wreck where the teenage driver sat, decapitated, but still holding the steering wheel; the little girl—the same age as your daughter—who you held in your arms as her rapist was taken into custody. Through all of these calls, day after day, you are required to remain calm. Professional decorum requires that you ignore your personal feelings, respond professionally, and just move on to the next call. But where do all those feelings—the anger, disgust, horror, and heartbreak—go?

Susan Lewis Simons, founder and director of Under the Shield, Inc., (http/www.undertheshield.com) presents the best analogy in *The Simons Theory of the Psychological Garbage Can.* This theory explains what happens to those unexpressed emotions and difficult experiences by comparing one's psyche to a kitchen garbage can. All the old, dirty, messy, nasty things that you shove into your garbage can at home are not unlike all the dirty, ugly mess you encounter on the job. As you go through your day, month, year, or career, shoving all that nastiness deep into this internal garbage can, it begins to fill up. How much messy gunk will fit in there? Probably quite a bit if, like most officers, you keep shoving it in and pushing it deep inside.

Eventually though, that garbage can cannot hold any more and begins to overflow. In the case of your psychological garbage can, it's going to overflow at inappropriate times and onto the wrong people. Keep shoving more garbage in and one day that garbage can will burst open, spreading that mess all over your life, your family, and your job. Just like at home, however, there is a simple solution to the overflowing garbage within an officer's soul—empty it before it gets full!

It is critical that you develop a support system and find someone to talk to about the hard stuff that builds up inside—a garbage collector, so to speak. It may be a friend, coworker, relative, pastor—anyone you trust and with whom you feel safe, someone who won't freak out about the stories and thoughts you share. Who do you have to fill that role? Siblings are sometimes good at this or maybe your old non-cop friend from high school. Frequently, a fellow officer or retired officer who has experienced the same things proves to be the best sounding board. That's where peer support groups come in.

You may have a local peer support organization in your area where active and retired first responders can offer confidential support and advice based on experience. Try searching for a group in your area or asking fellow officers. Under the Shield, Inc. is a national organization that provides guidance and support for and by current or former law enforcement and military personnel.

Wherever you find it, please don't hesitate to reach out for help should you ever need it. Nor should you underestimate the value of what you have to offer others who walk in your shoes. An off-duty connection to other officers can save a life, whether it be someone else's or your own.

## THANK YOU FOR YOUR SERVICE

I sincerely hope you hear that so often that it becomes cliché, but for too many of our officers, that is not the case. So let me say it again: Thank you! Thank you for serving, protecting, and defending. Thank you for saving us from ourselves and each other. Thank you for sacrificing so much of your life for those who seem to have so little understanding or appreciation.

I have on many occasions in this book and in my life, referred to you as heroes—even superheroes. Yet I've never met an officer who accepts that title comfortably. Nevertheless, to me and many others, most especially your mom, you are just that. In a world where the word "hero" is thrown about for sports figures and celebrities or a regular Joe who shows common courtesy, that term has lost much of its meaning. But there are still many people who remember what makes a true hero, and you show us what that word means each day. You still inspire little kids and bring a smile to those in pain. You do what is right because you believe the world can be made better. You protect and you serve, and you fight when you have to.

Thank you. And please stay safe!

# CHAPTER 16

# Being A Police Family

I hope by now you have recognized that police life, with all its highs and lows, is something you can live with. Though I hope you've come to realize that it's even more than that. To be inducted into a police family, voluntarily or not, is to be welcomed into a society populated by the best this world has to offer. We are special. You are special. Your LEO sons and daughters are special. We stand together along the Thin Blue Line, as the families who "Back the Blue." I hope you take pride in that. There is also some responsibility that comes with being a police family.

> *Behind every strong police officer there is an even stronger family who stands by them, supports them, and loves them with all their heart!*
> — ANONYMOUS

If we are to be that strength for all who need us, we have a responsibility to ourselves, our officers, and each other. We must take care of ourselves in every way—physically, mentally, emotionally, and spiritually.

Having lost my own mother many years ago, I can ask with

all sincerity, who will your family, your officer, have to lean on if you are not there? It is impossible for a spouse or anyone to replace you in your officer's eyes. So yes, do all those things you've been told over the years to take care of yourself physically. Eat well, exercise (best stress reliever *ever*), breathe deeply in the clean fresh air, and take care of those nagging physical ailments.

Continue to learn and challenge yourself mentally. Never say "I can't" because you never learned how to do something. Learn it. Stay abreast of current events. Read for knowledge and entertainment. Challenge yourself to do something new each month. Have meaningful conversations with people who know things you may not, and remember, that person may be your officer or others within your own family. Keep growing.

As we have discussed throughout these pages, this life is stressful for moms. Get the help you need to manage that and the many other stresses in your life. Whether it is through a morning meditation, a walk in the woods, lunch with friends, or visits with a professional counselor, find that thing (or things) that feeds your soul, calms your spirit, helps you cope, and gives you the strength to carry on for all those who depend on you.

## THE GOOD PART

Yes, there are good things about this life. We have focused so much on the things that cause you and your family to struggle, maybe you didn't hear me mention all the amazing, wonderful, fun-filled days you will encounter along the way. From the pride and excitement of that very first day, there will be occasions that make your heart soar and bring tears of joy. There are award ceremonies and promotions, news reports of children rescued, and stories told of lives saved—all featuring your officer. There will be police Family Days filled with fun and games, and community events where you get to represent your son's or daughter's department. Your heart will be filled with love for officers you've never met, and you will live for the smile you can bring to those who work with your son or daughter. And all along the way, you will find friendships that can change your life.

## THE SISTERHOOD BEHIND THE THIN BLUE LINE

As you go through life as a police mom, the most important thing to remember is that you are never alone. There are approximately 700,000 police officers in the United States alone, and my own rough show-of-hands research says that about three-quarters of them have a mom, alive and filled with pride and worries, just like you. There is no reason you'd ever be unable to find another police mom to connect with.

Reach out and find us. We are your sisters, and we are here for you, just as we ask that you be here for us. We're on social media and websites for all things police related. We're at your local precinct and community events. We're the moms of your officer's partners and coworkers, even your officer's supervisors. We've been waiting for you.

Welcome to the Family!

# APPENDIX A

## GLOSSARY

**10-Code** - A common form of communication used by some law enforcement agencies to describe a type of report or case or to communicate frequently used phrases. These codes may vary by department and are being phased out by many agencies. Examples of the more commonly used codes include:

**10-4**  Affirmative / Okay
**10-7**  Out of Service
**10-10**  Negative / No
**10-16**  Domestic Disturbance
**10-20**  Location
**10-22**  Disregard
**10-31**  Crime in Progress
**10-33**  Emergency / Officer Down

**Complement** - The number of officers that are required to fully staff an area, precinct, or department. Example: two patrol officers per ward, nine wards per precinct, resulting in a full complement of eighteen patrol officers to cover one shift in that precinct.

**C.O.P.S.** - Concerns of Police Survivors; a nonprofit organization that provides an array of services for families who have lost an officer in a Line of Duty Death.

**DEA** - Drug Enforcement Agency; a national law enforcement agency dedicated to combating drug trafficking.

**DV** - Domestic violence; often one of the most dreaded and dangerous calls an officer can respond to.

**EAP** - Employee Assistance Program. A network of mental health providers contracted by a law enforcement agency to provide services to officers at reduced or no fees.

**Final Signal C** - The term for the final time an officer will check out or go off duty, as in the case of an officer's retirement or death.

**FOP** - Fraternal Order of Police. The national union for law enforcement officers. Although they may have little responsibility in cities with their own unions, the FOP may be the active union for many officers across the country.

**Got Your Six** - A phrase used by police and military meaning "I've got your back." Derived from the traditional use of a clock face to describe direction. Six o'clock would thus mean behind you, or in back of you.

**K-9** - May refer to the unit as a whole or to the police dogs who are used by a department in a variety of ways, including drug searches, criminal apprehension, and search and rescue.

**LEO** - Law Enforcement Officer; refers to any sworn officer certified by a local, county, state, or national government agency.

**Motors** - The shortened and commonly used name for the motorcycle unit in any department.

**Mounted Patrol** - Officers who ride specially trained horses to patrol and participate in community events.

**Officer-Involved Shooting** - Any incident where an officer fires a weapon and either wounds or kills another person, usually a suspect.

**OJI** - On-the-Job Injury. Each agency or state determines what constitutes an on-the-job injury, with these parameters occasionally being called into question. Since financial compensation and benefits are tied to this designation of an officer's injury, the designation can carry high stakes.

**P2** - A rank or term for a Patrolman used by some departments referring to a fully trained officer who may be working in any number of positions within the department. May also be written as PII, using Roman numerals.

**P2P -** Patrolman 2 on Probation; an officer who has completed his training but still working on a probationary status. May also be written as PIIP.

**P2PT -** Patrolman 2 on Probation and in Training; usually referring to a new officer working with an FTO to receive on-the-job training. May also be written as PIIPT. Not every department will differentiate this status from a P2P.

**Patrolman -** The mainstay of any city or county law enforcement agency. These officers patrol their jurisdiction, respond to calls, direct traffic, work vehicle accidents, perform welfare checks, make arrests, testify in court cases, and much more. Sometimes referred to as a Patrol Officer.

**Precinct -** A geographic area of a city or jurisdiction where officers are assigned to patrol, usually with a physical police station within that area where officers report to work, attend roll call, do paperwork, pick up equipment, work out, and relax.

**Perp -** A suspect or perpetrator.

**PIO -** Public Information Office or Officer. This office handles public statements, press releases, and public relations for a department.

**POS** - A "piece of shit" suspect or criminal. Often used by officers in casual conversation, not in an official capacity.

**Probie** - Slang term for a new officer on probation.

**Recruit** - An individual in the police academy training to become an officer. May also be called a trainee.

**Rookie** - A new officer, usually referring to one in his probation phase but sometimes following an officer well beyond that time.

**Sea of Blue** - A procession of law enforcement vehicles, involving police cars, motorcycles, and special units, that drive a designated route in a stunning display of blue lights in honor of a fallen officer. Sometimes other first responder vehicles will participate as well.

**Signal C** - The term used to communicate that an officer is going off duty.

**SWAT** - Special Weapons and Tactics. A police unit specially trained and equipped to handle unusually hazardous situations.

**TACT** - Tactical Apprehension and Containment Team. Same as a SWAT unit.

**Ward -** A small geographic area within a specific precinct where an officer patrols and responds to calls. Officers may respond to calls outside their Ward and will always respond to a call across Wards when an officer needs assistance.

# APPENDIX B

## CHAIN OF COMMAND AND RELATED INSIGNIA

The Memphis Police Department uses these sworn personnel ranks, following the tradition of military ranks and other law enforcement agencies. Check with your officer to be sure these are the ranks, titles, and chain of command used in her department.

| Title | Insignia |
|---|---|
| Chief | (five stars) |
| Assistant Chief | (four stars) |
| Deputy Chief | (three stars) |
| Colonel | (eagle) |
| Lt. Colonel | (oak leaf) |
| Major | (oak leaf) |
| Lieutenant | (bar) |
| Sergeant | (chevrons) |

# APPENDIX C

## RESOURCES

### Mental Health

- **American Foundation for Suicide Prevention**
www.afsp.org
Dedicated to saving lives and bringing hope to those affected by suicide. Click on "Find Support" for help.

- **Badge of Life**
www.badgeoflife.org
Nonprofit organization website run by active and retired law enforcement officers. They produce a quarterly news-letter offering valuable information, advocate for yearly mental health checkups, and offer free training videos.

- **Code-9 Project**
www.code9project.org
Nonprofit organization that provides education, sup-port, and self-help to all law enforcement families to manage stress, reduce and eliminate PTSD, and prevent suicide. They produced an award-winning documentary, *Law Enforcement and Post-Traumatic Stress: A Deadly Combination* and they sponsor many events and work-

shops, including S.H.A.R.E., a two-day program for first responders and their families.

- **COPLINE – An Officer's Lifeline**
  www.copline.org
  800-COPLINE / 800-267-5463
  Nonprofit organization serving active and retired law enforcement officers and their loved ones, providing confidential services for callers who are dealing with various stressors both on and off the job. Trained and vetted retired officers are available 24/7 to listen and provide culturally appropriate resources.

- **First Responders Support Network**
  (415) 721-9789
  www.frsn.org
  This is NOT the same as the peer support group, Mid-South First Responders Support Network in Memphis, that is mentioned in the text of this book. It is, however, a highly rated program whose goal is to provide first responders and their families with tools to reduce the effects of traumatic incident stress. The key programs are the 6-day residential treatment for first responders, also known as the West Coast Post-trauma Retreat (WCPR), and the 6-day program for significant others and spouses (SOS). The FRSN is a collaboration of first responder peers (included but not limited to police, fire, corrections, dispatch, and emergency

medical services), SOS peers, culturally competent mental health clinicians, and chaplains who volunteer their time.

- **National Suicide Prevention Lifeline**
Nationwide Hotline: 988 (Available 24/7)
www.988lifeline.org
Free and confidential support for people in distress, prevention and crisis resources for at-risk individuals and loved ones.

- **Safe Call Now**
(206) 459-3020
Confidential, comprehensive, 24-hour crisis referral service for all public safety employees, all emergency services personnel and their family members nationwide.

- **Suicide Prevention Help**
www.suicidepreventionhelp.com
Provides advice on coping with suicidal thoughts or suicidal friends and loved ones.

- **Under the Shield, Inc.**
855-889-2348
www.undertheshield.com
Nonprofit organization whose mission is to meet the unique needs of law enforcement, fire service, emergency medical service, military personnel and their family mem-

bers by providing support through confidential services, education, and public awareness. Services are provided in an anonymous and confidential environment by trained current or former first responders, with coaching and training centered around The Simons Theory of the Psychological Garbage Can. Services include Peer Support, Stress Coaching, and Licensed Mental Health.

- **USA National Suicide and Crisis Hotlines**
  988 – Emotional support available nationwide (Available 24/7)
  800-273-TALK (800-273-8255)
  800-SUICIDE (800-784-2433) www.suicidehotlines.com/national.html
  Website offers crisis support, information, and state-by-state referral resources.

## Line-of-Duty Deaths

- **Blue H.E.L.P.**
  www.bluehelp.org
  It is the mission of Blue H.E.L.P. to reduce mental health stigma through education, advocate for benefits for those suffering from post-traumatic stress, acknowledge the service and sacrifice of law enforcement officers lost to suicide, support families after a suicide, and bring awareness to suicide and mental health issues.

- **C.O.P.S. (Concerns of Police Survivors)**
www.nationalcops.org
573-346-4911
Highly regarded national organization dedicated to helping the survivors of line of duty police deaths. They offer
peer support, legislative advocacy, information about
benefits, scholarships for surviving children, summer
camps for children, a regular newsletter, and National
Police Week Memorial activities. Chapters exist around
the country.

- **First Responders Children's Foundation**
www.1strcf.org
Provides financial support to children who have lost a
parent in the line of duty as well as families enduring significant financial hardship due to tragic circumstances.

- **National Law Enforcement Officers Memorial
Fund**
www.nleomf.com
This organization's mission is to increase public support
for law enforcement by commemorating those who have
died in the line of duty. Their website provides information about National Police Week and the National Law
Enforcement Museum.

- **Officer Down Memorial Page**

  www.odmp.org

  Nonprofit organization dedicated to honoring America's fallen law enforcement officers by preserving their photos, stories, and meaningful memories and reflections of those who love them.

## Officer and Family Support

- **FOP (Fraternal Order of Police)**

  www.fop.net

  The Fraternal Order of Police is the world's largest organization of sworn police officers and has chapters in most major cities and every U.S. state. They serve as the voice of those who protect and serve and are committed to improving the working conditions and safety of law enforcement officers through education, legislation, information, community involvement, and employee representation.

- **FOP Auxiliary (Fraternal Order of Police Auxiliary)**

  www.fop.net/about-the-fop/fop-auxiliary

  The Fraternal Order of Police Auxiliary, for families of the Fraternal Order of Police members, has chapters in many states. They advocate for law enforcement and offer programs for family health and safety, assistance and training for critical incidents, networking scholarships, and information regarding legislative issues important to police families.

- **Law Enforcement Family Resources**
  www.theiacp.org/icprlawenforcementfamily
  Information and resources for spouses, partners, parents, children, and companions of law enforcement officers provided by the International Association of Chiefs of Police.

- **National Police Wives Association**
  www.nationalpolicewivesofficial.org
  NPWA is a non-profit charitable organization dedicated to supporting law enforcement spouses through various outreach programs, providing resources to those new to the law enforcement community, as well as promoting volunteerism and charity within the law enforcement community in general.

## Advocacy Groups

- **International Association of Women Police (IAWO)**
  www.iawp.org
  Publishes a quarterly magazine, *Women Police*, and represents the interests of policewomen throughout the world, with members in 57 countries.

- **National Association of Black Law Enforcement Officers (NABLEO)**
  www.nableo.org
  Nonprofit organization representing the needs and concerns of law enforcement personnel of color, addressing those issues which have a direct impact, both adverse and positive, on the employment, promotion, and retention of minority law enforcement officers in every facet of the Criminal Justice system. They have over twenty chapters, primarily in the Northeast United States.

- **Out to Protect**
  www.outtoprotect.org
  Nonprofit organization with the mission of increasing awareness about lesbian, gay, bisexual, and transgender professionals working in law enforcement and offering support and guidance to those pursuing a law enforcement career.

## Facebook Support Groups for Moms, Parents, and Spouses

- **Moms of Police Officers (MOPO) Facebook Group**
  www.facebook.com/groups/1836260753060454
  Group is for mothers of police officers throughout the country. Private group and verification of your role as a police mom is confirmed; tight security in place to ensure the safety and confidentiality of our officers and

their families. This is a positive environment, with no politics, drama, or fundraising allowed. We are Blue Sisters here to support and encourage one another through the challenges and concerns of being the proud mother of an LEO. I am one of the administrators of this group and encourage you to join us.

- **Mothers of Police Officers (fmopo) Facebook Group**
www.facebook.com/groups/1537266249849236
Mothers of Police Officers who support the police and each other. This is a politically conservative group of moms who pray for all LEOs and each other and share their concerns together. Photo proof of your son/daughter is required to ensure you are a police mom.

- **MPD Moms 2.0 Facebook Group**
www.facebook.com/groups/4086151961420508
If you happen to have an officer serving on the Memphis Police Department, this is the place for you. Exclusively for mothers of Memphis Police Officers, whether you live local or across the country, we encourage you to join us. We are proud moms who support our officers and each other with strength and encouragement and we allow no politics or drama. We are friends and cheerleaders for one another and our officers. This is the group I founded in 2015 that started me down this path.

- **Parents of Law Officers**
  www.facebook.com/groups/916619642097989
  Moms and dads of law enforcement officers throughout the United States will find a network of other parents, useful information, and news about national and local incidents involving our officers. Attention is paid to honoring those officers injured or killed in the line of duty and helping parents cope.

- **National Police Wives Association**
  www.facebook.com/NationalPoliceWivesAssociation
  Website: www.nationalpolicewivesofficial.org/
  This organization provides support to those needing assistance and understanding. Connect with police spouses around the country and learn about the various programs and resources for those new to the law enforcement community while supporting one another.

## Recommended Reading:

- **Bullets in the Washing Machine**
  Littles, Melissa (2011)
  The founder of the popular blog, *The Police Wife Life*, provides a light-hearted look at the humorous and positive aspects of living life as a law enforcement spouse.

- **Emotional Survival for Law Enforcement, A Guide for Officers and Their Families**
  Gilmartin, Kevin M., Ph.D. (2002)
  Order online at www.emotionalsurvival.com
  The premier book for help understanding the emotional well-being and behaviors of police officers throughout their careers. A must-read for every law enforcement officer and family. If you read only one book throughout your officer's career, let it be this one!

- **His Badge, My Story, Insights for Spouses and Loved Ones of Law Enforcement Officers**
  Gustafson, Vicki (2019)
  Based on the author's three decades as a law enforcement wife, she shares suggestions and guidance to help others become independent, strong, and brave enough to face the worry and fear of a law enforcement family.

- **How Heroes Heal**
  Marilyn Wooley (2022
  True stories of psychologically-injured first responders – and their transformation from wounded warriors to victorious heroes. This book offers a pathway toward recovery and growth, helping first responders get to the other side of trauma, learning how to function better than before, so that they not only survive, but thrive.

- **I Love A Cop: What Police Families Need to Know**
  Kirschman, Ellen, Ph.D. (Third Edition 2018)
  This is a valuable resource that cops and their loved ones can rely on for practical advice from a police psychologist and volunteer clinician at the First Responder Support Network. Covers issues pertinent to police wives and other family members, including relationships, trauma, domestic violence, alcohol abuse, home life, and other difficult topics, with no-nonsense guidance to help your family thrive.

- **Increasing Resilience in Police and Emergency Personnel: Strengthening Your Mental Armor**
  Stephanie M. Conn (2018)
  Illuminates the psychological, emotional, behavioral, and spiritual impact of police work on police officers, administrators, emergency communicators, and their families. It debunks myths about weakness and offers practical tips for police employees and their families struggling with traumatic stress and burnout.

# APPENDIX D

## LEO GIFT SUGGESTIONS

I've been asked so many times for gift ideas for those special occasions in a police officer's career—graduation from the academy, promotions, or retirement—it seemed like a good idea to share some suggestions here.

### Academy Graduation:

Note, not all departments provide all the gear—or the best quality gear—an officer will need to perform their duties and come home safe. These first few items may be vital to his job. Just be sure that any equipment you give as a gift is approved by his department and meets his needs.

- Backup Gun – Departments usually provide a list of approved models.
- Kevlar Vest – "Tactical" or "weight-bearing" vest or heavier plates to go in his vest.
- Boots – Ankle support and good traction are essential, as are comfort and fit.
- Heavy Coat and Rain Gear – Usually specific to the department and purchased through the uniform store they use.

- Pocket knife – Size and type usually dictated by the department.
- Handcuffs – Officers and departments may have preferences on type.
- Flashlight – Different styles for different purposes.

## Throughout His or Her Career:

At graduation or throughout his or her career, these items are useful or meaningful for any officer.

- Under Armour Cold Gear – pants, shirts, socks, etc.
- Cooling t-shirts – moisture-wicking or the newer cooling fabrics
- Protective gloves
- Ear warmers or stocking cap
- Off-duty police themed apparel St. Michael pendant, coin, or visor clip
- Pocket notebook cover Pen that writes in the rain and in any direction
- Car carrier for all the gear they have to transfer in and out of the patrol car
- First Aid kit for personal vehicle or patrol car
- Additional tourniquets to be carried on the uniform
- Gear Rack to hold duty belt and other equipment at home
- Challenge coin display case
- Police-themed wall art or figurine

- Police-themed car decals
- Session with a tattoo artist for a police tattoo

## Retirement:

Retirement gifts can be practical, humorous, or sentimental; all are appreciated as an officer leaves a career of great highs and lows and moves toward his next chapter in life.

- Shadow box containing patches, badge, and other items depicting his career
- Framed photograph or newspaper article of a significant moment in his career
- "Retired Cop" apparel, figurine, or art

# APPENDIX E

**National Law Enforcement Appreciation Day – January 9th:** Sometimes referred to as L.E.A.D, it was created in 2015 by several organizations that came together to show appreciation for police officers following a rash of police shootings and hatred. Common ways to show appreciation for officers on this day would be to shine a blue light on your front porch, fly a blue ribbon from your car antenna or mailbox, wear blue clothing, and turn your Facebook page blue for the day.

**National Police Week – Week of May containing the 15th:** National Police Week is celebrated in whatever week **May 15, National Police Officers Memorial Day,** falls. This decree was signed in 1962 by President John F. Kennedy to honor the men and women who have lost their lives in the line of duty. It is a time when police officers honor their fallen colleagues and ensure those surviving them are supported. Citizens can also celebrate the day by showing their gratitude to police officers in the community. National Police Week is about honor, gratitude, remembrance, and support. Many departments hold local ceremonies to honor those lost during the preceding year and their families left behind. The highlight, however, is the weeklong event held in Washington, DC, culminating in a candlelight vigil.

**National Thank an Officer Day – 3ʳᵈ Saturday in September:** This day is set aside each year to honor those who protect and serve throughout our nation. There are many ways to participate, not the least of which is to actually say thank you to any officer you see. Other ideas include sending a thank you card to your local police station or precinct or having a stack of cards to give to individual officers throughout the day. You might also take small goodie bags (gum, hard candies, granola bar, hand sanitizer, small spiral notebook, blue line sticker, etc.) to officers at your local precinct, or perhaps pay for a meal for officers in a restaurant or coffee shop when you see them.

# NOTE FROM THE AUTHOR

I hope you found this book helpful and will keep it handy to refer back to anytime the fears take hold, new challenges arise, or you need to be reminded that you are not alone.

I always enjoy hearing from other police moms. Feel free to contact me with questions and feedback, or just to introduce yourself and tell me your story. I can be reached via my website at www.policemoms.com or by email at policemom901@gmail.com.

Remember, we are always, *Stronger Together!*